T0334090

Cambridge Elements ≡

Elements in Forensic Linguistics
edited by
Tim Grant
Aston University
Tammy Gales
Hofstra University

THE LANGUAGE OF ROMANCE CRIMES

Interactions of Love, Money, and Threat

Elisabeth Carter

CAMBRIDGE
UNIVERSITY PRESS

CAMBRIDGE
UNIVERSITY PRESS

Shaftesbury Road, Cambridge CB2 8EA, United Kingdom

One Liberty Plaza, 20th Floor, New York, NY 10006, USA

477 Williamstown Road, Port Melbourne, VIC 3207, Australia

314–321, 3rd Floor, Plot 3, Splendor Forum, Jasola District Centre, New Delhi – 110025, India

103 Penang Road, #05–06/07, Visioncrest Commercial, Singapore 238467

Cambridge University Press is part of Cambridge University Press & Assessment, a department of the University of Cambridge.

We share the University's mission to contribute to society through the pursuit of education, learning and research at the highest international levels of excellence.

www.cambridge.org
Information on this title: www.cambridge.org/9781009500418

DOI: 10.1017/9781009273008

First published 2024

A catalogue record for this publication is available from the British Library.

ISBN 978-1-009-50041-8 Hardback
ISBN 978-1-009-27299-5 Paperback
ISSN 2634-7334 (online)
ISSN 2634-7326 (print)

The Language of Romance Crimes

Interactions of Love, Money, and Threat

Elements in Forensic Linguistics

DOI: 10.1017/9781009273008
First published online: March 2024

Elisabeth Carter

Author for correspondence: Elisabeth Carter, Elisabeth.Carter@protonmail.com

Abstract: Exploring the interplay of love, money, and threat in romance fraud, this Element reveals how language is used to persuade, manipulate, and threaten without causing alarm. It provides the first empirical examination of criminal interactions-in-action that exposes and tracks the grooming process and manipulation techniques from first contact with the fraudster to the transition between romance and finance, and requests for money and intimate images, before morphing into explicit threats and acts of sextortion. Through the use of a range of interactional methodologies and real romance fraud messages, a new type of criminality in the form of 'romance fraud enabled sextortion' is revealed. The insights contained in this Element have clear implications for future directions of academic exploration and practitioner efforts to protect the public. This title is also available as Open Access on Cambridge Core.

Keywords: romance fraud, sextortion, interaction, coercion, forensic linguistics

ISBNs: 9781009500418 (HB), 9781009272995 (PB), 9781009273008 (OC)
ISSNs: 2634-7334 (online), 2634-7326 (print)

Contents

Series Preface

The Elements in Forensic Linguistics series from Cambridge University Press publishes across four main topic areas: (1) investigative and forensic text analysis; (2) the study of spoken linguistic practices in legal contexts; (3) the linguistic analysis of written legal texts; (4) explorations of the origins, development, and scope of the field in various countries and regions.

The Language of Romance Crimes: Interactions of Love, Money, and Threat responds to the first of these topic areas, but unlike some previous Elements in this area it focuses on the detailed description and analysis of this forensic genre, rather than directly on investigative techniques per se. Carter not only brings into public view valuable data that is rarely seen in the forensic linguistic literature, but her discourse and conversation analyses provide insights that frame the romance fraud conversations as a form of grooming. Indeed, although there are differences, there are also direct reads across in the language behaviours described by Carter and those described by Lorenzo Dus and colleagues in their Element on *The Language of Online Grooming* discourse in the context of child sexual abuse. One benefit of framing romance fraud as a crime that is achieved as a result of grooming is that it has the potential to mitigate the impact of the victim blaming that is seen in some media reports of this kind of abuse – that seems to suggest that only sad, lonely, stupid people would become a victim of this kind of offending.

Overall, this Element provides a thorough and important exploration of romance fraud and makes a strong contribution to tackling this significant crime type. It should be read not only by linguists with interests in the area, but also by psychologists, criminologists, and readers from other related disciplines.

Tim Grant
Series Editor

1 Introduction

Exploring the interplay of love, money, and threat, this Element reveals the inner workings of romance fraud. Drawing on real interactions between romance fraudsters and their victims, it exposes how language is used to persuade, manipulate, and threaten without causing the victim alarm. Indeed, as romance fraud is a crime where the active cooperation of the victim is required in order to successfully defraud them of their money, it is essential for the victim to be an unsuspecting and willing participant. This Element examines how fraudsters' early requests and demands are legitimised and normalised within the guise of romance by criminals intent on exploiting that interaction for financial gain. It provides the first empirical examination of how fraudsters' interactions with victims become successful in requesting money and intimate images, videos, and conversations without causing alarm, and how these then morph into explicit threats and sextortion.

Romance fraud is a pervasive crime that is one of the UK's most commonly experienced crime types. It sits within the offence of 'fraud by false representation', which involves 'a person dishonestly and knowingly making an untrue or misleading representation of themselves in order to make a gain for themselves, or cause loss to another or to expose another to a risk of loss' (definition adapted from the Fraud Act 2006, s2). At the time of publication, fraud constitutes 41 per cent of all crime in the UK, costing victims £1.2bn in 2022 alone, of which £31.3 million was taken from victims as a result of romance fraud (UK Finance, 2023). However, as victim reporting rates remain low (an estimated 15 per cent, Crime Survey for England and Wales 2019), these statistics clearly grossly underrepresent the scale and financial consequences of this crime type. Romance fraud is a crime type where the perpetrator engages with an individual with the intention of defrauding them of their money. Despite its categorisation as a type of 'advance fee fraud' (Action Fraud 2023a, 2023b), defined as 'when fraudsters target victims to make advance or upfront payments for goods, services and/or financial gains that do not materialise', romance fraud is in fact distinct from these types of fraud. Advance fee frauds include holiday fraud and online shopping fraud which involve payment being elicited for goods and services that do not exist, whereas romance fraud typically involves a protracted period of communication prior to requests for money. Such requests are posed within the context of an established relationship that has been developed for that very purpose, with no promise of goods or services; rather, the continued relationship is the only draw. Romance fraud can occur over many months or years as it relies on the establishment and development of trust and belief by the victim that the relationship is genuine, and it is that very trust that is then exploited for criminal financial gain (Buchanan and Whitty 2013), with the emotional bond itself obscuring from the victim the financial abuse that ensues (Anesa 2020).

Victims of romance fraud, whether there has been financial loss or not (Whitty and Buchanan 2016), experience a unique harm. Besides the financial harm, the psychological impacts of romance fraud have been described as so egregious as to be akin to the psychological harm experienced by rape survivors, or as a type of death (Whitty and Buchanan 2016), and can lead to death by suicide as a direct result of the fraud (Button, Lewis, and Tapley 2014; House of Lords 2022). Impacts of victimhood ripple out to families of victims (Button, Lewis, and Tapley 2014). Despite the high-harm nature of this crime and its pervasiveness as the most common criminal act in UK society, fraud remains on the periphery of academic endeavour in the social sciences. Much of the research in this area is psychologically driven and focuses on victim suscepti- bility, vulnerability, and reasons why individuals have experienced a failure to protect themselves from fraud. These range from impaired cognitive ability (Judges et al. 2017), cognitive errors (Alicke and Govorun 2005), being dis- tracted by greed, errors of judgement (Anesa 2020), errors in decision-making (Lea, Fischer, and Evans 2009), and an addictive nature and impulsivity (Whitty 2018). Social isolation has also been identified as a factor that drives continued contact with those known or suspected to be defrauding them (Yuxi et al. 2022), as has the absence of a capable guardian (Kennedy, Rorie, and Benson 2021) to protect and temper unwise decisions. There are indeed factors that increase vulnerability in a legal and social care sense (Hawkswood, Carter, and Brown 2022) or situational vulnerabilities, such as a recent bereavement, job loss, or financial and health-related precarities (Dove 2020), which then in turn translate to a decreased resistance to responding to fraudulent approaches. However, through a tide change in research in this area, understandings are becoming clear that there need not be a vulnerable individual for the crime to take place. What is needed is a criminal who is intent on committing fraud and a human being to receive a communication from them; focusing on what the victim has or hasn't done to protect themselves drives the focus away from the perpetrator and contributes to victim-blaming discourses. This Element reveals and con- textualises how the overall structure of romance frauds and the language used within them accommodate a range of desired outcomes. Through its empirical analysis of real romance fraud interactions it provides a uniquely in-depth perspective on the mechanisms of these intimate and devastating crimes as they twist from the first flush of love all the way to explicit threats to life.

Reflecting general misunderstandings of fraud as a crime, and mirroring academic focus on victim behaviour as a cause of their own victimhood, current public-facing 'protect' messaging (that is, information, awareness raising, and education designed to protect the public from becoming victim to fraud or from continuing in a fraudulent interaction) relies on the (mis)understanding that fraud is a crime much like burglary, where a perpetrator's criminal actions can be easily identified if spotted 'on the job', and the public can, and should, protect themselves adequately enough to not be a victim (much like ensuring windows are locked). The focus on demands for money, particularly when they are represented as 'out of the blue' and/or 'from a stranger' do not represent the reality, where often the focus on romance means the fraudster is considered anything but a stranger, and requests are not surprising or jarring but are embedded well within the romantic context. The romantic context also serves to disguise requests for money so they aren't necessarily recognised as such and are not the main focus of the interaction (Offei et al. 2022). Requests for money can also be disguised and mitigated by being recast as something else: a short-term loan, an investment, or a joint enterprise. The entire act of requesting can be disguised so well that victims can feel compelled to offer money to the fraudster and feel that it was their decision (Carter 2021), meaning the financial abuse is not recognised by the victim as such at all.

By misrepresenting the reality of fraud as a series of distinct and discrete types of theft akin to burglary, and not as multifaceted and intertwining types of grooming and abuse (Carter 2023), the public that these messages are designed to protect are provided with a false sense of security that they will easily be able to identify fraud and protect themselves from it in a simple and highly effective manner. Those who do then become a victim of fraud experience the shame of not having been able to perform the ostensibly simple task of self-protection and blame themselves for their victimhood. The shame associated with becoming a victim of fraud is reflected in the chronically low fraud crime reporting rates (Button and Cross 2017). This simplification and misrepresentation of fraud as a crime, fraud protection, and impacts of victimhood perpetuate society's negative narratives of fraud victims: that they are complacent, greedy, stupid, or in some way cognitively compromised (Cross 2015). Further, individuals who are currently in a fraudulent relationship often experience denial of the situation they are in (Whitty and Buchanan 2016) that prevents reporting and may itself be an effect of fraud protection messaging not enabling victims to see their situation as unsafe and one they should leave immediately. Denial also causes victims of fraud to be vulnerable to repeat victimisation as they do not report or seek support as victims of a crime (Whitty and Buchanan 2016).

Whitty (2018: 105) describes this as a 'double hit' – a financial loss and the loss of a relationship, going on to say that 'for some victims the loss of the relationship was more upsetting than their financial losses, with some victims describing their loss as the equivalent of experiencing a death of a loved one'. This is due to the modus operandi of this crime relying on building trust and using the guise of a romantic relationship in order to use that trust and love to harm the victim, who then has to come to terms with the fact that the person they believed to be their long-term partner was only doing that to defraud them of their money; they have lost the money and their partner. Often this leads to impacts on self-esteem, independence, and shame. This is supported by recent work that explores the language and the effect of language used in fraudulent communications, as well as the behaviours of perpetrators of domestic abuse and coercive control (Carter 2023). The findings reveal similarities in aspects of grooming, isolation, compelling secrecy, encouraging self-blame, and distort-ing the reality of victims in both domestic abuse (Domestic Abuse Act 2021, s1;

Victim Support 2023) and coercive control (Serious Crime Act 2015, s76; Crown Prosecution Service 2023).

Compounding this, victims of romance fraud can also be coerced into performing what amount to serious criminal acts themselves, such as money laundering via becoming a money mule, while under the belief they are legally transferring money to, or on behalf of, their loved one (Anesa 2020). Beyond the direct fraud itself, victims can also experience ongoing fear for their online and offline personal safety and fear of further victimisation through identity theft (Cross and Lee 2022). Fenge and Lee (2018) discuss the profound negative impact of scams on personal health and wellbeing as a public health issue. Victims of fraud are also left vulnerable to being targeted for further frauds based on their status as a fraud victim, such as recovery fraud. This is where fraudsters pose as police officers or other officials to manipulate prior victims of fraud into complying with requests for money, under the guise of asset recovery (Action Fraud 2023c). This exposes the exploitation of an individual's status as a fraud victim as a commodity to be bought and sold for other criminals to exploit. Further harms that victims of romance fraud are exposed to include sextortion, blackmail, and, crossing the digital–physical divide, kidnap (Cross, Smith, and Richards 2014).

The National Crime Agency definition states that sextortion is 'webcam blackmail' (NCA 2023), describing the offence as 'financially motivated sexual extortion', where 'criminals might befriend victims online by using a fake identity and then trick them into performing sexual acts in front of their webcam' (NCA 2023). Extorting money from the victim is understood to be the sole purpose of the interaction, which is usually brief and abruptly ends at the point at which the intimate images or video are captured by the perpetrator. However, the issue of financial reward for the perpetrator is not an essential component of the crime in Walsh and Tener's (2022: 1) definition: 'threats to expose a sexual image in order to make a person do something *or for reasons such as revenge or humiliation*' (emphasis my own). Indeed, located as it is within 'kidnap and extortion' rather than 'fraud' (NCA 2023), sextortion is not actually considered an economic crime. This legal separation of fraud and sextortion leads to the interactional mechanisms used by criminals in coercing intimate and explicit communications from victims during romance fraud being hidden, and as a fraud typology entirely unknown. The siloing of fraud and sextortion also leads to uneven data access opportunities available for academic research, criminal investigations, and to inform police protect and prevent strategies, due to the sensitive nature of crimes within 'kidnap and extortion' such as kidnappings, trafficking, hostages, and ransoms. This explains the dearth of empirical research into the language of these crimes. It disguises their interlinked and often co-produced nature, driving protection guidance to represent romance fraud as a singular criminal episode, and leaving the public under-protected from sextortion attempts embedded within the 'relationship'. This Element cuts across these legal and conceptual tramlines for the first time to provide the first in-depth examination of how fraudsters arm themselves with images and messages sent to them by the victim during a faux romance with the express intent of weaponising them against the romance fraud victim they are currently communicating with. This Element will show how, in the context of romance fraud, sextortion occurs as an offshoot or additional act of criminality that is initiated during, and occurs after, a longer-term interaction where trust has been built and the victim believes they are in a genuine romantic relationship with the perpetrator. It reveals how when the facade of the romance fails, if the fraudster has garnered personal details or intimate content from the victim during its course, they can move on to direct threats now designed to frighten rather than subtly convince the victim into taking action. Indeed, during the course of writing this Element it became apparent that it uncovers an as-yet-unknown aspect of this criminality – termed here for the first time as *romance fraud enabled sextortion*, which is different in modus operandi, traditional understandings and definitions of sextortion.

The high-harm nature and impacts of fraud on individuals have been discussed earlier in this section; the impacts of sextortion on individuals' wellbeing and mental health have also led to suicidal thoughts and deaths by suicide (Nilsson et al. 2019; O'Malley 2023). By examining where these two crimes not only interlink, in terms of interactional techniques by the perpetrators, but also how they coexist and rely on one another in the performance of the offences, it becomes abundantly clear that the impacts of *romance fraud enabled sextortion* are wholly devastating.

In the following sections, interactions at each stage of the romance fraud journey are identified, presented, analysed, and discussed, from the start of the romance, the transition to financial requests, the finance stage and, finally, post-romance, where the grooming of the romantic relationship ends and the sextortion and direct threats begin. This Element is the first of its kind to document these stages, reveal in 'real time' how they happen, and expose the linguistic tools used by fraudsters with the anticipation of successfully grooming and defrauding the victim. In doing so it represents an opportunity to drive forward academic and practitioner understandings of fraud as a crime, providing tools for evidence-based practice that better protects the public from this crime type. Each element of the romance fraud journey is presented in date order, and numbering within the extracts is for ease of reference in terms of analysis and discussion when drawing attention to a particular part of an extract.

The numbering doesn't necessarily reflect the stage of the interaction in terms of how long it has been being going on for. However, where there are two or more extracts being drawn on in a discussion and their relative position in the wider interaction is of importance or a contextual location would be useful, the numbering is used to reflect the gap between extracts in terms of the number of turns taken. The data comprises seventy-one extracts from thirty romance fraud cases, provided by the victims with their informed consent and university ethical approval. The seventy-one extracts have been chosen as representative moments across the corpus in the romance fraud journey to show the reality of romance fraud interaction in action. The interactions across the corpus are representative of romance frauds in terms of broad content and interactional tactics, and the findings from this research can be used to make recommendations in terms of fraud protection and prevention strategies, as has my work to date. Due to the difficulty in accessing cases that include sextortion, resulting from the lack of a reporting mechanism that captures sextortion within romance fraud, together with the compounded shame associated with romance fraud and sextortion victimhood preventing reporting in these cases, these have been drawn from publicly available sources which, with permission from the victims, publish their correspondence with fraudsters. These are more often presented with no or little content from the victim as this has been redacted at the request of the victim. In all extracts, formatting, punctuation, and spelling are retained from the original messages and names and any other identifying information have been anonymised or removed from the interactions. In cases of removal, the fraudster is referred to as F and, where present, the victim as V.

Critical discourse analysis and principles from conversation analytic theory are used to explore the criminal interactions between fraudsters and victims. Critical discourse analysis is used to examine fraudsters' discursive practices in context, exposing these in relation to the use of identity and power to facilitate manipulation of the victim, while conversation analytic principles are used to explore the development of the back and forth between fraudster and victim, situating the fraudster's tactics as part of the talk-in-action. These interactions are grouped, as explained earlier, into the stages of romance, transition, finance, and post-romance sextortion. It is, however, important to note here that not all romance frauds end in sextortion; rather, in many romance frauds, assisted by the context, attempts are made to elicit intimate messaging and/or images, and only the successful attempts in doing so are then harnessed by the fraudster through sextortion when the romance fails to yield financially. The interactions will reveal how language is used to define and progress the relationship within that element of romance fraud while manipulating and persuading victims, balancing the need to avoid causing alarm or victim withdrawal from the interaction. Each of these four stages enables the analytic focus on a particular part of the romance fraud journey from the early building of rapport through to a more established romance, a partnership involving financial dealings, the complete distortion of that relationship, and finally to where the criminal now delivers explicit threats. The analytic section identifies and examines the various guises and manifestations of fraudsters' implicit and explicit 'calls for action' within the sub-areas of this crime in action, and how the push and pull of these calls are driven by methods used when the existing method becomes, or appears, less productive or unfeasible. The analyses focus on the ways in which language is used by fraudsters to create a facade of romance, and then how they transition between romance and discussions relating to financial needs and requests before finally segueing into direct sextortion. The analysis of the fraudsters' correspondence first explores what interactional tools are drawn upon to establish their own credibility as a genuine romantic prospect, and then how they broach the topic of money and manage both states relating to romance and finance, respectively. It then focuses on the transition from a romantic overture to attempts to coerce, and then threaten, the victim into sending money.

This Element exposes the reality of romance fraud from the first contact in order to reveal how ordinary it can be, and how it develops from that initial conversation and morphs into situations that may, in isolation and without context, seem extraordinary. However, when situated within the long-term grooming that romance fraud involves, it becomes clear how victims make what they feel are reasonable and ordinary decisions given the relationship and the context. Throughout, there will be insights into the ways in which the findings could be used in public-facing protection literature, guidance, and education in order to accurately represent fraud, provide effective ways to deliver self-protection suggestions, and to assist those already in a fraudulent relationship. This Element proposes the introduction of more effective protections for the public, representing victims of fraud as victims of grooming and not as subjects of ridicule. This will encourage reporting, which will in turn assist in driving academic and practitioner understandings of the scope and impacts of fraud. The following section opens a series of detailed analyses of romance fraud interactions, beginning with the early communications encapsulated in the 'romance' stage.

2 Analysis

Romance

This section explores how fraudsters establish credibility and trust and build rapport, before developing the manipulation through scripting expectations, harnessing religion, forecasting and normalising future behaviours, and normalising risk-taking. As romance fraud occurs within the guise of a relationship, rather than a one-off communication as in postal frauds (Carter 2015) or a financially focused interaction colloquially known as 'pig butchering', it is necessary for the fraudster to sustain the facade of genuine communication for an extended period of time, often over many hundreds or thousands of interactions with the victim. By way of example, Avery and Mandy interacted over 14,000 times over a six-month period, Adam and Carly 1,134 times over a month, and Roger and Camilla over 88,000 times over the eleven-month course of their communication. After convincingly performing the business of starting a romantic relationship, the fraudster therefore needs to develop and maintain it within that facade for extended periods of time. As such, successful romance frauds require the perpetrator to engage in interactional techniques that support both the aim of establishing credibility as a genuine individual and the practical business of successfully engaging and developing a romantic relationship. Then they move on to attempting to defraud the victim, where this shift in focus also needs to be managed within the bounds of the romantic relationship.

Gaining victim compliance with requests that will defraud them or leave them open to later exploitation (through giving fraudsters personal details, intimate communications, and money) is the ultimate aim of the fraud. However, to ensure compliance, fraudsters need to mitigate, normalise, or otherwise hide concerning requests within the romance through reducing 'social and communicative differences' (Giles 2009: 278). Maintaining rapport and consent from a participant in an interaction while the other interactant has a different motivation can create 'relational tensions' (Spencer-Oatey 2002: 542) that need to be managed, more so when the motivation of one party has negative consequences for or requires impositions on the other. In romance fraud, the process begins in a similar way to how 'addressing immediate concerns' (Carter 2015: 91) is performed in postal frauds. The opening interactions of perpetrators of romance fraud contain a variety of discursive tools designed to establish their credibility through addressing and also diminishing recipient concerns around the potential that the other interlocutor might be a fraudster. These tools are grouped into two broad categories: implicit and explicit addressing of early concerns.

Addressing Early Concerns – Implicit

Vulnerability is established early on as part of the initial set-up for the fraud to come (Carter 2021). This is legitimised through genre mapping (Carter 2015), an interactional tactic in which the fraudster will leverage the facade of the developing romance to perform displays of vulnerability as part of rapport building through the exchange of personal information. By revealing their vulnerabilities, fraudsters give victims a sense of control, which implicitly supports the fraudster's credibility by mitigating general (mis)perceptions of the power differential in relation to the potential threat of the person they are communicating with. Part of appearing to be a credible romantic prospect is the demonstration of possessing the quality of being safe or non-threatening. This is performed in fraudulent relationships by the fraudster manipulating the power balance by appearing vulnerable or by distancing themselves from the archetypal dating site danger of being a fraudster; the following extracts demonstrate these techniques in action. By discussing personal circumstances, particularly when this involves revealing information that may make them a less attractive dating prospect, the fraudster presents a facade of honesty and openness that is the antithesis of a fraudster desperate to con a mark.

One type of vulnerability is inexperience – being a novice on the dating site enables the fraudster to present themselves as non-powerful, non-expert, and with little or no experience: a non-threatening position that implicitly evokes an innocent persona which is the antithesis of bad actors who spend a lot of time on the site and are well experienced in attempting online dating. By showing a willingness to be vulnerable and show his inexperience, James' narrative in Extract 1 is couched in the wider narrative of mitigation and caution; 'to be honest' (lines 1–2) serves to indicate his newness to the site as information he is revealing to the victim, and 'it's better' (line 3) refers to it being better for him, given his newness to the site, that they do not meet until they get to know each other.

Extract 1
1.   James: I am relatively new to this whole concept of internet dating to be
2.   honest and i think its better, knowing that we can keep
3.   communication here over the email until it gets to meeting in person,
4.   I am a caring, honest and God fearing man …

By sharing his feelings around meeting up front, the fraudster is performing a type of 'set-up' (Carter 2021), whereby he introduces information that he will later rely on in the conversation as facts, evidence, or mitigations. That these are introduced early on in the relationship as part of contextually appropriate talk means that these interaction points remain innocuous, appear genuine, and don't attract the scrutiny or concern they would otherwise do if accompanied, for example, with a request for money, or produced as an excuse in response to a victim asking to meet.

Another type of vulnerability that is produced as part of the fraudster's manipulation toolkit is the pretence of having been hurt in a previous relationship.

This situates the fraudster in a position that is couched in caution and concern about the safety of the current interaction, which places the victim in a position of responsibility over the fraudster's feelings. Managing this contextual vulnerability serves to draw the victim into focusing on ensuring they do not inadvertently cause the fraudster harm through their own communications with them, and away from querying the authenticity of the person they are interacting with. Amplifying this, much like in the pretence of vulnerability through inexperience, this vulnerability through prior hurt has encoded within it the assumption of credibility, as someone revealing they have experienced harm at the hands of an online relationship is antithetical to the experience of a perpetrator of online harms.

In Extract 2, following the victim's (Julie's) suggestion to take the relationship slowly, the fraudster (Peter) responds by hoping she doesn't hurt his feelings. This is a type of what I've termed 'trauma bombing', where the fraudster increases the emotional stakes or references to traumatic situations and/or the impacts of these, in order to distract from the reality of the situation (an ask for money or letting the victim down). In this extract, we can see the fraudster beginning to use trauma bombing to take control of the conversation; it is no longer about her wishes; from line 2 it becomes about his concerns, in particular around her future behaviour.

Extract 2
1. Julie: Are you happy to take things slowly and see where it leads us?
2. Peter: Yes off course Julie am ready to take things slowly and hope you
3.   don't hurt my feelings

This is a type of power play where Peter ostensibly agrees with Julie's preference for taking the relationship slowly, but directs this agreement towards his wishes, through which the onus falls on the victim to 'live up to' these expectations of the ideal partner and avoid harming the fraudster.

In the following quote, Dan draws on a fabricated past situation in which he had committed to marrying a woman only to find out that she was being unfaithful ('Three weeks to my wedding I caught my fiancé cheating with my close friend'). This narrative is useful for the fraudster as it sets up the idea that he may have trust issues and behave in ways that would otherwise be interpreted as concerning, such as requiring information on his partner's location and activities, and in asking for shows of trust from her, such as sending him money. The fact that he couches the discovery of his fiancé's vulnerability as 'catching her in the act' and that this was with his friend both serve to deepen the emotional toll on the fraudster that he can then harness in future interactions, whereby the victim will be compelled to seek ways to reassure him that this relationship is different.

Vulnerability is also established through other situations out of the fraudster's control that are outside of the dating sphere: 'ever since i lost my late wife it has [not] been too easy for me' (Peter). Claiming to be a widower enables the fraudster to weave the narrative that he has a dependent child (useful as a way to bond with a victim who also has dependents and to leverage when asking for money), without the negative connotations and additional complications of having an ex-spouse.

Another type of vulnerability is based around reliance, demonstrated by the following claim that 'a man is reduced to nothing except he has someone to call his own. am so glad i have you . . . thanks for being there' (Dan). This moves closer to discourses more commonly associated with coercive control and domestic violence and abuse; the fraudster manufactures a situation where the victim is in a position of power and control relative to the fraudster, but the burden of responsibility they feel for keeping the fraudster safe and well, and to avoid hurting them, makes it difficult for them to leave the relationship or (as we see later) refuse requests for money.

Both of these examples draw on themes of loneliness and nothingness, a void that is gladly and gratefully filled by the communications of the victim but will return if she leaves. Extract 3 makes mention of the frequency of the victim's (Mary's) contact and how her 'keeping in touch daily' (line 3) is important in keeping James' loneliness at bay.

Extract 3

1.	James:	I want you to know that all i need is your love and honest..caring
2.		and humble self. I am really glad to read from you and i am getting
3.		used to you and keeping in touch daily also, and it make me happy
4.		every time i read from you, it means we keeping each other in mind, i
5.		am glad this is happening to me at this time of the year because i
6.		have been so lonely and hopefully with you i wont have to be alone
7.		any more.

James enhances the relevance of her actions and adds a sense of urgency to them by aligning them with his current situation and feelings at that time of year, making her continued efforts in communicating daily with him important right now and into the immediate future. Vulnerability is also used by fraudsters to directly address concerns of their authenticity and credibility, and to present a facade of a casual attitude towards the relationship as a foil to revealing the opposite reality, and this is what is explored in the following section.

Addressing Early Concerns – Explicit

The following extracts show fraudsters distancing themselves from the identity of being a fraudster by situating themselves as vulnerable to the advances of fraudsters (they are posed as the 'other'), offering advice to guard against fraudsters and making their negative opinion of fraudsters clear. The techniques such as demonstrating knowledge and authority (but not aggression) seen here are also used to build rapport in other, genuine interactions such as debt collection phone calls (Harrington 2018). Additionally, in fraudulent contexts the act itself of directly or indirectly mentioning fraudsters creates a facade of credibility; by themselves drawing attention to the presence and possibility of fraudsters, liars, and cheats on the dating site and elsewhere, they implicitly demonstrate themselves as *not this*, and distance themselves from anyone who is, together with reinforcing their own openness and honesty, as shown by the following quote:

Extract 4
 James: I don't lie, cheat deceive or steal and I do and not associate with those who do.

James also explicitly disavows himself from controlling behaviour, the type of behaviour that is typical of abusive relationships:

Extract 5
 James: I am not the controlling type.

In Extract 6, the fraudster Peter is explicit in distancing himself from 'others' (line 1) that may not be sincere. This is reinforced by the second half of his turn where he makes his promise to come to the UK more tangible by mentioning plans to have dinner with Julie ('home' in this context is meant to mean Julie's home).

Extract 6
1. Peter: Julie i am interested in you don't mistake me for others because
2.   everything is coming out from my sincerity heart and will love to have
3.   dinner date with you as soon as i return back home

The transition from abstract to concrete continues in his use of 'will', which shows certainty; and the use of 'return' and 'home' frames Peter's visit to Julie as respectively an inevitable homecoming and to a place where he belongs, rather than a temporary visit. The use of 'back' is perplexing as he has not previously visited Julie's house; however, this is understood as a reinforcement of the facade of permanency and staking a claim to her home as his home. This narrative in its entirety is at odds with the reason he gives for his visit – to have their first dinner date.

In Extract 7 we see the joint and mutual recognition of the dangers of online dating in terms of attempts to defraud. The fraudster Dan positions himself as 'other' than fraudsters and, as someone who has been defrauded when online dating previously, familiar with the potential dangers in online dating and keen to make her aware of the dangers and protect her from them. This increases his facade of credibility and trustworthiness, positioning him as 'not one of the dangers', similar to the tactics used in postal frauds (Carter 2015). He explicitly brings up having been in a potentially fraudulent relationship he escaped from recently without giving the person money.

Extract 7

1.	Dan:	You have to be careful
2.		Was talking with one woman earlier but she stopped talking to me
3.		because I refused to give her more money for her travels
4.	Peggy:	Very careful. I have had the same experience on another website – the
5.		guy wanted £10 k as a deposit for a hospital operation in Germany
6.	Dan:	Hope you didn't give any
7.	Peggy:	No but the language when he realised he wouldn't get anything was
8.		not good. Had 5 contact me who were scammers so have nothing to
9.		do with that website now
10.	Dan:	You really have to be careful

The eagerness Dan has to educate Peggy about the dangers of fraudsters in the online dating space is reflected in his use of the imperative 'you have to' (line 1). The close repeat of line 1 and addition of 'really' on line 10 reinforces and emphasises Dan's message and its importance, his apparent sincerity, and his position of knowledge and protection. Interestingly, Dan details that he had already parted with money ('I refused to give her *more*', line 3) and contrasts this on line 6 with 'Hope you didn't give *any*', demonstrating a learning experience on the part of Dan and positioning him as speaking from authority on the matter.

In Extract 8, under the guise of offering protective advice, the fraudster (Dan) shows the victim (Peggy) how he is also vulnerable to being targeted by 'weirdos' (line 4), showing he is experienced but also vulnerable. He distances himself from unsavoury characters on the dating site, of which there are 'lots' (line 4), positioning himself together with Peggy as both new to the dating site and on guard against unsavoury characters.

Extract 8

1.	Dan:	Tell me how long have you been on dating site
2.	Peggy:	Oh a very long time – 3 days! And you
3.	Dan:	About a week now
4.	Dan:	Lots of weirdos on there

The word choice 'there' in relation to where the 'weirdos' are distances both him and Peggy from the dating site; using 'there' rather than 'here' fuels an implicit move for the two of them to go to a safer place. It is a typical M.O. of romance fraudsters to move their intended victim from the dating site and into personal messaging in order to escape protections on the site and inhabit a space where they can access the victim 24 hours a day.

Distancing themselves from being a fraudster can also be performed more subtly through displaying a lack of urgency and a more casual attitude towards the relationship and its fate. As shown in Extract 9, introducing the possibility that the relationship won't work and wanting to 'take things slowly' shows an openness and a lack of threat, desperation, or hidden mission associated with trying to defraud someone, much like the fraudster's explicit openness to doubt about their written communications (Carter 2015). This also works to draw the victim into trying to make the relationship work as there is a possibility that the other person will not continue with it, which makes the relationship seem more precarious and sought after.

Extract 9

1.	Stuart:	Hi Viv, how are you doing ? thank you for the lovely email, its so nice
2.		to hear from you. I am excited we are taking things slowly in the
3.		process of getting to know each other. I like the feeling as i have not
4.		felt like this in a long time. My heart tells me it could be you but i
5.		don't want to jinx it but hopefully time will tell. I enjoy reading your
6.		emails and writing you but there is much more to a relationship than
7.		reading and writing but i am glad we are on the right path and so far
8.		so good, we are also on the same page.

The phrase 'it could be you' on line 4 positions the fraudster in a powerful, decision-making role and the victim in the role akin to auditionee for his love, looking to win the coveted part of girlfriend, if she fits his requirements. Famously used as an advertising tagline in the UK for the National Lottery (1997), 'it could be you' evokes an all-powerful 'other' seeking out the lucky one-in-many-millions who will win the jackpot. The use of 'hope' alongside this evokes a sense of fate, chance, opportunity, and luck in being the 'chosen one'. Stuart continues by praising Viv's communications but tempering this with the use of 'but', which introduces caution and potential conflict to the current situation; he mentions future non-specified additional requirements (potentially intimate messaging) that will also need to be satisfied for the relationship to continue. Embodied in Stuart's 'so far so good' (lines 7–8) is the precarity of the current situation, and the victim will prove herself the right match for him based on her actions.

This is continued in Extract 10 with 'even if things don't work out' (lines 2–3), which reinforces the credibility of the interaction – not all meetings online develop into a relationship. It again reinforces the credibility of the fraudster as a legitimate love interest as it is assumed that someone intent on defrauding another for their money wouldn't willingly invite and risk prematurely ending the relationship that is the conduit for that goal.

Extract 10

1.	Stuart:	I never thought I will be this happy again, I just pray for long life for
2.		us both as I believe we are meant for each other and even if things
3.		don't work out i believe we can still be very good friends who will
4.		always be honest with each other and who will always be there for
5.		each other.

Stuart's orientation to the longevity of the relationship, whether it continues as a romance or as a friendship, ensures that the exploitation can continue regardless of relationship status; this serves as a type of 'future-proofing' of the relationship beyond its current status, a type of fatalism that ties the victim to him in a connection framed as mutual. This has echoes of the duty and responsibility often felt by victims of domestic abuse, cultivated by the perpetrator to offer little escape from its clutches (Hill 2020). During this, Stuart also takes care to script that future relationship, in whatever form it becomes, as one where they have a duty to 'be there' for each other (line 4), which is reminiscent of the 'set-up' (Carter 2021), in a narrative of assistance through which future requests for money can be couched.

Building Rapport

Rapport building is essential in romance fraud, as it is in any genuine developing relationship. This is in part why romance fraud is so pervasive and hard to spot; its protagonists use communicative frameworks that are expected and normal for the beginning of legitimate, genuine relationships and so do not raise 'red flags' or sound 'alarm bells' that would give victims cause to question or cease the interaction. Indeed, the converse is true – the normalcy of seeking personal information that would be concerning in other, non-relationship-based communications makes these interactions 'safe'. Beyond this, anyone who refuses to engage in these most basic rapport and relationship-building communications will be unlikely to progress past the early stages of an online relationship. Indeed, such refusal to reciprocate is considered unusual, and individuals who are very protective of their personal information and history could be considered worthy of concern as a result of their guarded behaviour. Public-facing fraud protection literature does tell us that fraudsters will seek information from their target victims but will not reveal information about themselves (Sussex Police 2023).

The information that is ideal for extorting a person's money is the same type of information exchanged between individuals in a genuine love match; occupation, location, age, marital status, family status, pets, loves, fears and so on can all be used by fraudsters to create a false reality that resonates personally with the victim, which in turn will make them feel safe and listened to, develop feelings for the fraudster and be more likely to perform what is asked of them later in the relationship. A solid foundation of rapport and trust will enable victims themselves to ignore or explain away 'alarm bells' or 'red flags' through the distortion of reality-driven confirmation bias, making assumptions of trustworthiness based on themselves as trustworthy and the fraudster being like them. By building rapport, fraudsters develop and establish a facade of credibility that enables them to earn the trust of their target. They are able to deliver messages to them that distort their reality, grooming them into accepting and normalising otherwise concerning behaviours later in the relationship.

Scripting Expectations

Setting out expectations is where the fraudster starts to develop the manipulation by being more explicit and prescriptive in detailing the victim's role in the relationship, although this remains couched within the norms of the 'getting to know you' building of a relationship so that it doesn't cause alarm. Seemingly ordinary expectations of the relationship, laid out as part of the building of rapport, bonding, and finding out about each other, are subtly manoeuvred beyond expectations of their ideal partner into qualities ideal for enabling an exploitative relationship. This is also directed towards servicing ideals around taking risks and supporting partners, useful to support or normalise later requests for money. The fraudsters in Extracts 11, 12, and 13 also leverage reciprocal acts within the context of romance.

In Extract 11, Peter uses the analogy of walking through fire (line 1) to describe the lengths that he would want his partner to go to for him (and he for them), and implicitly suggests future risks and difficult times they will need to talk through together. This is reinforced by the mention of sharing and problem-solving (line 3).

Extract 11
1. Peter: I want someone who will walk through fire for me and I would do
2.   the same for them. (Not literally ... but you know what I mean)
3.   share is problem solve and hope you are aware of that?"

Extract 12 shows James making his case even more explicitly, stating to Mary that 'my Ideal woman should try think the same way I do' (line 1), and 'She must love me only' (line 4). The fraudster continues by listing his desired behaviours in a partner and framing these in relation to his own behaviours (line 3). He also frames these behaviours in relation to mutual reciprocation, giving, sharing, and supporting him ('love me ... as I would love her', lines 10–11, 'be there for me ... as I will ... be there for her', lines 7–8).

Extract 12

1.	James:	My Ideal woman should try think the same way I do, be intelligent,
2.		someone who is willing to help share and build our dreams together,
3.		be as devoted to me and the family as I would be to her and conduct
4.		herself with poise and dignity. <u>She must</u> love me only as I would love
5.		her and accept that I will treat her like my queen, ensuring that she
6.		has everything her heart desires because If she is happy then I am
7.		happy. <u>I need</u> her to support and understand my work and be there
8.		for me when I need her as I will always cherish and be there for her

In Extract 13, Stuart also draws on the quid pro quo aspect of balancing a relationship while harnessing the angle that compromise and communication is down to ability and capability, and therefore in the gift of anyone who tries hard enough.

Extract 13

1.	Stuart:	My dream is to meet someone who will be able to communicate
2.		with me effortlessly. The ability to make compromise and grow is
3.		what I call true love. A man and woman must be able to find a happy
4.		medium. Being there for each other in good times and in bad times is
5.		very important. I appreciate a good turn and i also believe that one
6.		good turn deserves "millions of favors".

The final line of this extract lays bare the reframings and reciprocal notions on which later requests for money could be based – the victim as 'being there' for him in bad times (line 4), and mention of a 'good turn' and 'favours'. However, thankfully, in this case, he doesn't get to use this set-up later on to defraud Viv of her money, as the relationship stops after he sends two almost identical emails and doesn't respond to Viv's refusal to proclaim love or engage in love talk until they meet.

Scripting: Storytelling, Self-disclosure, and Disguising

Fraudsters harness false narratives of honesty and vulnerability styled as genuine self-disclosure to deliver messages of their credibility and harmless-ness within the normative framework of information sharing and rapport building associated with a developing romantic relationship. This is used to house and disguise the true nature of the interaction, enabling the fraudster to explicitly present a facade of honesty and safety without it looking out of place or causing concern to the recipient, encouraging reciprocal trust (Carter 2015). Indeed, as such narratives are expected within the early days of a relationship, their presence therefore implicitly reinforces the genuine nature of the inter-action, while in reality serving as the vehicle through which to extort and defraud.

Extract 14 shows the fraudster (Stuart) delivering a narrative about being honest and as someone who does not lie. This is seated within the wider discourse of being open to being questioned, which performs the task of the performance appearing open and the fraudster having nothing to hide. As well as the explicit statement of honesty, this turn also delivers this message implicitly through inviting the recipient to question him.

Extract 14

1. Stuart: Feel free to ask me anything you want to know about me. I welcome
2.   questions. You will always get my honest answers because lies are not
3.   worth it. They only lead to a cycle of deception. Enjoy your weekend.

This performance of honesty is also apparent in storytelling narratives, through which the fraudster delivers an account of who they are and their expectations of who they want the recipient to be. This interactional scripting enables fraudsters to detail how they want the victim to behave, while normalising these otherwise concerning behavioural demands often seen in coercive control and domestic abuse. Housed within the guise of honesty and self-disclosure, this scripting of the recipient's expected current and future behaviours is mitigated and non-threatening. It is performed as within a normal and mutual exchange of practical likes and dislikes that occurs in an open way as an unproblematic way to quickly assess mutual suitability and compatibility at the outset of a potential relationship.

The below quotes (Extracts 15–19) highlight honesty as a key requirement in the fraudsters' early interactions with their target victims. James and Dan start out by framing honesty and trustworthiness as essential qualities in terms of attractiveness and preference in a partner and in building a relationship.

Extract 15

    James: Someone once said " Truth can run naked and lies have to be covered " I try
    to live by it. I'm looking for someone who's honest, and Trust worthy.
    Without the Solid Foundation of Trust and Honest, No relationship can be
    built

Extract 16

    Dan: Tell me your turn on and turn off? Dishonesty turns me off the most

They both continue with descriptions of the qualities they rate most highly and what they are looking for in a partner:

Extract 17

    James: I'll like you to know that i prefer a honesty in my woman than any other
    Thing

Extract 18

> Dan: All I want in a woman is honesty, love and care

Extract 19

> James: I am looking to meet an attractive, intelligent, honest person who likes to have a good time and is fun to be around with.

In genuine relationships, this then precipitates mutual and reciprocal self-disclosure from both parties, known to be an important building block for trust (Mesch and Beker 2010). However, although the victim does reciprocate with their own self-disclosures (which in itself is useful for the fraudster to gather personal information about the victim), fraudsters also harness this interactional framework in order to produce their own version of self-disclosure *for and on behalf of the victim*; this involves telling them their qualities and what type of person they expect them to be. These descriptions are flattering, and as such both increase the victim's feelings of solidarity with the fraudster (Freiermuth 2011) and disguise the fraudster's scripting behaviour (Carter 2015). This scripting of the victim's assets is a type of 'set-up' (Carter 2021) of information that is used later to compel the victim to 'live up' to these originally flattering (and as such, uncontested) descriptions and romantic ideals, and then twisted into promises and agreements that, if not fulfilled, are recast as the victim undermining the relationship. Extract 20 shows the fraudster making a positive assessment of the victim's personality and qualities and weaving this into his future expectations of her.

Extract 20

1.	Stuart:	You really are everything I could possibly ask for in a woman. I am so
2.		impressed with your kindness and passion for life. You are very
3.		intelligent yet down to earth. Most of all, you are a beautiful woman
4.		and will continue to remain beautiful to me as we grow old together.

This is framed as a statement of discovery, reflecting the fraudster's transition from narratives of supposing and hoping to knowing as he gets to know her; this reinforces the perception that their relationship is developing, yet the flattering 'observations' exert pressure on the victim to 'live up to' a particular standard now and into the future.

Scripting of behaviours also enables the fraudster to direct the victim towards behaviours that will be beneficial when they later attempt to defraud them. This is another type of 'set-up' (Carter 2021) that occurs very early on in the relationship under the guise of rapport building. In Extract 21, Stuart outlines his desire to avoid drama in a relationship and for his partner to be faithful to him and value his love.

Extract 21

1.	Stuart:	I am a very happy man but i want to be happier. There is nothing in
2.		this world that would make me happy as much as having a drama free
3.		relationship. I would like to be with someone who understands love
4.		and knows what love is, Someone who is not ready to play with my
5.		heart, Someone who will value my heart when I give it to her.

This has implicit undertones of requiring loyalty. It is something that can be used as a tool to compel the victim into carrying out behaviours they would usually disagree with, with 'valuing' the fraudster's heart morphing into not disagreeing with him and doing what he says. The theme of the fraudster making explicit that he does not want the victim to 'play' with his emotions or engage in emotional 'games' is present in both in Extract 21 and in Extract 22. In the following quote we can see the fraudster using self-scripting to transmit his relationship expectations to the victim.

Extract 22

James: I am not a player and I do not go for head games.

These expectations are to remain faithful to the relationship as a serious entity and contribute to it consistently (not a player), and to be open and straightforward to requests and needs (no head games). This is the antithesis of a fraudster, who in order to deceive the victim must engage in 'head games'. As this is not a genuine relationship and there are many such victims, being a 'player' is part of the requirement of defrauding individuals through pretending to be in a romantic relationship with them. The illusion of self-expectations is that it presents an honest and trustworthy facade while also encouraging reciprocal self-scripting and behaviour in the relationship to which the fraudster can then hold the victim to account later if they are not generous, selfless, and private.

Scripting: Harnessing Religion

The use of God or religion in narratives within romance fraud enables fraudsters to engage in a type of 'othering' where the relationship itself is credited as part of fate, part of a wider design planned by someone other than them. This enables the fraudster to play the part of the narrator and joint participant, appearing removed from the driving force of the relationship and occupying a position alongside the victim as one of two people destined to meet. The fated nature of the relationship enables the othering of responsibility for them meeting and also additional responsibility for the two protagonists (with the victim bearing this responsibility) in terms of ensuring the will of the higher power is met and the relationship is a success.

In Extract 23, the fraudster credits God for orchestrating their love match and positions the victim as destined and designed to be there for the fraudster. This skews the power relationship and sets out the roles and expectations of the victim. This increases the difficulty, or completely obscures the ability, of the victim to challenge the authenticity of the relationship, as this challenge would then be directed at God and His will.

Extract 23
    James: you are my perfect person and i am grateful to God for bringing us together..

The objectification of the victim is again seen in Stuart's message in Extract 24, where Viv is described as a 'gift' that has been delivered to him, from the universe, for his benefit.

Extract 24
1.   Stuart: Sometimes I truly become convinced that this is merely a dream, and
2.   that in a blink of an eye, I would meet with you and have you in my
3.   arms. Its a blessing to me and I want you to know that you are just
4.   like a Gift from the universe to me and you have come into my life at
5.   the right time. I just want you to know that meeting you is a Blessing.

Such references also align the fraudster with the positive moral and ethical stance associated with someone who is religious, which is used as a way that fraudsters alleviate concerns around their credibility as the person on the other end of the conversation in online dating (Koon and Yoong 2013). It is in this way that religion is also harnessed as an indicator of trustworthiness: 'I consider myself loyal God Fearing and honest to a fault' (James).

This agenda also minimises perceptions of risk, as it embodies protection through the idea that if the relationship is destined to work then it cannot go wrong, and also the victim is encouraged to not stand in the way of destiny by avoiding risks. Success in a fraudulent relationship will ultimately be bound with displays of such 'commitment', joint *efforts* to ensure its success, and *sacrifices* in order to do so; all involve the victim and the transfer of money or goods, or personal information. This mirrors the interactions of call centre debt collection professionals, who frame that (legitimate) interaction as a joint effort in order to build and maintain rapport in the face of often unwanted requests of the recipient (Harrington 2018). The romanticisation of risk-taking to set up, situate, and normalise otherwise unpalatable requests as part of the context of romance fraud is addressed in the following section.

Forecasting and Normalising Future Behaviours

Scripting victim behaviour not only occurs throughout the development of the early stages of the fraudulent relationship through building rapport and laying out expectations, but at this stage it is also directed towards other ends. It is also used to romanticise the victim engaging in risky behaviour in the future, as well as normalising and contextualising concerning requests from the fraudster by situating these expectations and requests within the normalised framework of a developing relationship. This type of scripting is successful when romance and relationships are portrayed as the main cause of and justification for these behaviours. When so much of one's personality and self-esteem is wrapped up in whether a relationship is successful or not ('am I good enough?'), the intrinsic motivation is to comply with romantic expectations and relationship ideals and the ideals of the other party when they are too seated within that framework. This has echoes of coercion insofar as the victim often feels they are responsible for the success of the relationship, and not complying then becomes twisted by the fraudster into blaming the victim for not being committed enough or failing in some way.

Normalising Risk-taking

Personal fraud protection advice and warnings are often given alongside the idiom 'if it looks too good to be true, it probably is' (Gov.uk 2021; Metropolitan Police 2023), exposing the close link between fraud victimisation and risk-taking. As with all interpersonal or authorised push payment fraud, the fraudster requires and relies on the target individual's compliance in order for them to move their money. Intellectualising, mitigating, and justifying risk-taking is a powerful part of the fraudulent actor's toolkit in order to convince a target victim to act in ways that may be out of their comfort zone in order to defraud them (such as in romance fraud, investment fraud, and courier fraud) or incentivise them to act to secure a 'good deal' (such as in holiday fraud and online shopping fraud).

In the context of romance fraud, risk-taking is introduced early on in the relationship by the fraudster who harnesses tropes around 'risking it all for love' and 'love conquering all' to not only normalise taking risks, but also portray risk-taking as a desirable act that embodies heightened passion and romance.

In Extract 25, James explicitly addresses the topic of risk-taking with Mary, where it is presented as moving their relationship from a friendship into a romantic relationship.

Extract 25

1.	James:	I have so much respect for our friendship/relationship and what we
2.		are trying to build and i hope you feel the same way too, if you were
3.		just to give me one chance, I could show you that it could be amazing.
4.		You wont be hurt if you give me the chance to.. I just want you to
5.		take a risk and see how good it would feel to love. It always feels
6.		good to be in love am sure you also know that..I know that things
7.		could never be the same again but that's what life is about . . . taking
8.		risks! I could make you so happy. There's more to life than just sitting
9.		around waiting for something to happen; life will then just pass us
10.		by.

James opens the topic by talking about their continuing relationship. He categorises it as a 'friendship/relationship' (line 1), acknowledging that it is in the early stages and hasn't yet developed into a romantic interaction, but is building and is based on respect. James presents this moment as a crossroads in their relationship, one where if Mary chooses to pursue love, she will not regret it. He acknowledges Mary's reticence around developing the relationship romantically, topicalises this as a fear of being hurt, and on line 4 addresses this by promising her she won't be hurt. Once a practical element preventing risk-taking is addressed, James then moves on to more abstract concepts around risk and love, anchoring these on existing experiences of love that Mary may have felt and can therefore identify with – 'It always feels good to be in love am sure you also know that' (lines 5–6). As part of this risk-taking framework, fraudsters also draw on narratives of their willingness to risk or trade money for love, foregrounding self-sacrifice as a show of love and commitment.

As part of the narrative Dan in Extract 26 attempts to draw information from the victim about her financial status, using the tag question on line 1 to draw confirmation from her that she is indeed wealthy from a lifetime of work. This talk targets older adults, increased life experience and wealth being associated with retired older adults, and in implicitly leveraging the prospect of loneliness, which is a common concern among this age group (Cross 2016). Peggy's response shows that she is not in agreement; the use of 'well' (line 2) signals her dispreferred response to come (Heritage 1984), which is a partial rejection of Dan's turn by disagreeing with the notion she is wealthy. After that attempt fails, Dan launches another attempt to compel agreement from Peggy. He moves his focus from 'wealth' to 'excess': an important change in focus as excess is meant here as any money beyond the essential (eating, shelter, daily fun; lines 11–12). He frames having anything beyond the essentials as a negative and that people need to free themselves of, as it 'leads us to vanity' (line 12).

Extract 26

1.	Dan:	We have worked so hard and attained some wealth right?
2.	Peggy:	Well not sure about wealth but I have worked hard
3.	Dan:	i believe older women are experienced and committed in a
4.		relationship
5.	Dan:	But for what purpose? To be realistic, except if you just want to be
6.		known as a rich person, wealth means nothing if you have no one to
7.		share it with.
8.	Peggy:	True. I am a typical scorpion and if I commit it's for life
9.	Dan:	I believe you x
10.	Dan:	All the millions are useless indeed. how much do we need to eat?
11.	Dan:	How much do we need for shelter? how much do we need for daily
12.		fun. excess and excess leads us to vanity.
13.	Peggy:	I will tell you all about me in the email. I do need enough money to
14.		survive and have always lived within my means and agree all money
15.		but no love in your life is bad news
16.	Peggy:	I need to go to bed now
17.	Dan:	But for few of us who value the simplicity of life, we would do well
18.		in finding happiness
19.	Dan:	As i always say, money can buy a good bed, but never will money buy
20.		sleep. Money can buy sex, but can NEVER buy love. That is why, as
21.		my own man, i would give up all that can be bought for that which
22.		cant be bought.

He draws on her responses which indicate she isn't wealthy (line 2) but also lives within her means (line 14) to manoeuvre his narrative from talk of millions of pounds to aligning himself with her mindset and situation ('us', line 17), and in claiming ownership of a similar mindset that 'value[s] the simplicity of life' (line 17). He then harnesses these points to 'sell' happiness (at a price) as the missing element in her life. His attempts to align his talk with hers and gain agreement on this point are also shown through his adoption of her turn 'I need to go to bed now' (line 16), which, although a clear signal that she does not want to continue the conversation, is used by Dan on lines 19 and 20 ('money can buy a good bed, but never will money buy sleep') as a way to continue holding the floor and make his next turns relevant (if only on a lexical level).

Dan then issues the statement 'i would give up all that can be bought for that which cant be bought' (lines 20–21). Although he isn't asking Peggy to use her money in this way, Dan is setting up the idea early on in the relationship that this type of financial sacrifice should be considered acceptable in order to avoid loneliness and to attain love and happiness, and that this is a decision born from independence and not from thoughts of interference from others ('as my own man', lines 20–21).

Both of these points – love is worth sacrificing your money for, and these decisions are independently made – are important when it comes to later requests for money and accompanying demands for secrecy. The theme of sacrificing money for love is drawn on in Extract 27 when, only twenty-seven days later, he asks Peggy for money and she refuses, and he turns to threats in response:

Extract 27

> Dan: you value money material things more than love and life and will make sure
> you get yours soon

The following section explores the transition between the early stages of the relationship and the fraudsters' introduction of behaviours that move and prime the interaction into one where requests for money will later be introduced. In doing so it examines secrecy further, alongside urgency, which is another commonly concerning request, and how these and other behaviours are mitigated within the context of a supposedly romantic relationship.

Transition

Mitigating otherwise concerning situations or requests (for secrecy, urgency, inability to meet or engage in video calls, for personal information or photos) not only enables these to occur but also normalises the future, ultimate mitigations made by the fraudster when they initiate and follow through on financially damaging requests. These situations are the ones that are styled as the 'red flags' or that should set off 'alarm bells' in individuals who find themselves on the receiving end. Here I examine how the fraudster mitigates these requests via claims and denials through which broader tactics of encouraging urgency and secrecy are often drawn on to enable the fraudster to encourage the victim to act without thinking through the options, as well as for the grooming to remain undetected by sources of support.

Normalising Secrecy

Requests for secrecy are also normalised by the fraudster through their own enactment of the behaviour they want from the victim. This is another type of 'othering', where demands and requests are performed non-directly or implicitly by others by referring to others, or in this case through the actions of the fraudster establishing a behavioural norm. In Extract 28, Dan explains why he has kept information about a contract from his close family, framing this as something that can be done later once the situation is resolved. This is a type of 'set-up', where secrecy is normalised ahead of requiring it of the victim in relation to financial requests of them to come. This normalises secrecy through his performance of it himself, an action that, if later performed by the victim, would be ideal for the fraudster in terms of enabling the victim to be groomed without external support or assistance from family or friends who could, as parties separate from the grooming, identify the interaction as illegitimate.

Extract 28
1. Dan: Didn't tell my sister and mum about my contract here,so they don't
2.   make unnecessary demands lol, i need that home first

This interaction also evidences the fraudster's narrow range of options in terms of who they can draw on for support, increasing the pressure on the victim to deliver that support. The fraudster implicitly demonstrates that his interaction with the victim is more open than with his close family. This also enhances the facade of the fraudster having a strong bond and level of trust with the victim, as she is party to information that his close family are not.

In Extract 29, Emmanuel performs a similar task in framing his discussion with his cousin as confidential and the act of talking to others about their relationship as unusual and an invitation for 'people to meddle'. The use of communication with a third party is another example of othering, as he is recounting a conversation and using this as a tool to set the boundaries around sharing information with others rather than directly telling the victim to not discuss the relationship with others. This ensures the demands for secrecy remain non-confrontational and appear as part of an aside rather than something essential to the 'relationship', both of which would likely cause concern to the victim or cause them to question this.

Extract 29
1. Emmanuel: I wanted to give you wonderful news.
2.   I talked over the phone to my cousin Petra
3.   (confidentially, as we don't want, do we? people to meddle
4.   unless we wanted them to),
5.   and she is so mightily impressed with you,
6.   and so delighted for us, that she offers
7.   the wedding, and offers to organise it herself!
8.   You see, Donna, humankind does have
9.   the milk of lovingkindness in it.
10.   Please tell you mum, to make her, too, happy!
11.   Love, my wonderful Donna!
12.   Emmanuel

His use of 'we' (line 3) situates this perspective of keeping their relationship secret as a jointly agreed relationship quality. This is important because, as well as the othering discussed earlier, this framing of the secrecy as jointly agreed also serves to mitigate concerns. It disguises the one-sided demand for secrecy as a mutual part of the relationship. The tag question 'do we?' (line 3) offers the illusion of control to the victim, ostensibly asking if this course of action is ok with her, but in reality it acts as a rhetorical question as it is 'wonderful news' (line 1).

Normalising Requests for Personal Information

Fraudsters' requests for personal information from the victim sets them on the journey towards financial abuse. In a modus operandi similar to the 'foot-in-the-door' technique (Anesa 2020: 5), once a victim provides personal details, it becomes a matter of small, additional, incremental steps towards providing other details, such as bank account details. In Extract 30, the fraudster uses the details provided by the victim to send a series of communications framed as from the diplomatic service and United Nations, communications that reinforce the credibility and legitimacy of his story and future requests that then involve money. That these details were ostensibly used for the purpose detailed in Extract 30 provides positive reinforcement and paves the way for future requests. However, this can be far from an innocuous provision of information; email addresses, home addresses, and telephone numbers are valuable data that can be exploited (Wang and Topalli 2022) by being sold to other fraudsters (Button, Lewis, and Tapley 2009), which itself constitutes an indirect financial gain from fraud victims. Additionally, procuring these details from the victim also exposes them to future threats after the romance has finished; Extracts 67, 68, and 69 later in the Element show fraudsters directly leveraging their knowledge of the victims' address in order to extort money from them.

Extract 30

1.	F:	Darling I just had to find a way to write you this message. The captain & the
2.		Coast Guards here in the Island ordered that everyone should make sure we
3.		don't have any valuable with us if we must proceed on our journey that
4.		everyone will have to find alternative means of transporting or securing their
5.		things, that every alternative transport material or security items must be
6.		found.
7.	F:	Honey, I have my business Credentials. We understand that there are
8.		specialized maritime security companies here on the coast of the island, and
9.		at this point you need to be with me. I have decided to send my personal
10.		(business) life documents quickly so you can help me secure them until I get
11.		home to meet you
12.	F:	Darling, you need to give me the following information quickly: your full
13.		names. Your home address, your mobile phone number and your e-mail
14.		address. This is the only information I will provide to the diplomatic firm so
15.		they can contact you when they are ready to deliver.

By drawing on his need to complete an urgent, protective task (the sending of important documents to a safe place amid a crisis) that involves only an administrative action from the victim distorts the perceived risk involved as it is the fraudster that implicitly frames themselves to be trusting the victim with their important information and documents, and not the other way round. This is reinforced by the gravity of the context (an urgent situation involving the United Nations and the diplomatic service). The request is weighted towards eliciting agreement rather than refusal due to the nature of the need for the details and the urgency ('you need to be with me' / 'you can help me' / 'you need to give me', lines 9, 10, 12) with which they are requested.

In Extract 30, risk is also tempered through the limitation on the information the victim needs to send ('this is the only information I will provide', line 14), together with fraudster's use of 'everyone, you, me and us' throughout the extract in relation to his description of the situation through the fraudster's orientation; this concerns the entire crew on board, who also need to do the same.

In Extract 31, the fraudster's reasons for wanting the victim's banking information moves from administrative 'I want to save this in my jotting book' (line 6), to love bombing (Strutzenberg 2016) through elevating his status from boyfriend to husband (line 9) and harnessing the relationship as a tool through which to compel her to provide the details.

Extract 31
1. F: So tell me do you have your new account now set ??
2. V: Yes I do
3. F: Oh ok
4. F: I wish I can know your new bank details. You didn't give it to me.
5. V: No need to
6. F: No let me know darling. I want to save this in my jotting book
7. V: I don't give those details out
8. F: I'm aware darling.
9. F: But you forgot I'm your husband? Not just an ordinary person
10. V: When you're here
11. F: Come on. . Do I look like a stranger
12. F: I get worried and sometimes feel you doubt me and my personality.
13. V: Why do you need them
14. F: Just wanted to save them As I have the first one there.

The narratives used when leveraging the relationship involve addressing the victim's move to protect her personal details ('I don't give those details out', line 7), but claiming his status means that he isn't someone she needs to guard her details from ('like a stranger', line 11); he is inside her private sphere and sits outside of such self-protection requirements. He then uses this to produce a visceral response in relation to the effect this denial has on his mental health (she makes him worried, line 12, he feels doubted, he feels his personality is in question), a recognised technique used by fraudsters to draw a protective response and compliance from their victims (Carter 2021).

He then returns to his claim he would like to save the details, using 'just' to minimise the relevance of the details, and then framing having the details as only because he wants to save them as he has the previous details. While implicitly minimising the importance of having the victim's bank details, the fraudster also directs attention away from the fact he could use them for financial gain while also referring to the fact that she had agreed to give him her bank details previously, implying that this is no different and not a risk or concern to repeat the same on this occasion.

Normalising Requests for Photos and Initiation of Intimate Messaging

Sharing personal information and physical contact is part of building and continuing a romantic relationship. Online relationships are now commonplace, and this accelerated in no small part due to the Covid-19 pandemic. As part of this, the development of intimacy transposes into writing personal details and sending intimate photos and videos to someone, with these activities having become a normalised part of relationship building.

Much like requests for money, the request and exchange of intimate photos, videos, and messages is represented as a clear 'red flag'. However, within healthy online relationships, discussions and agreements in relation to sharing intimate photos and videos and engaging in sexual acts on camera and through messaging can mark the development of a relationship to the 'next stage', signalling mutual trust, desire, and the satisfaction of sexual urges through the online medium that the relationship is currently bound to. Within this contextual framework, the request for intimacy takes place in the only way it can – through visual and audio means. This is therefore not an alarming request as it is not out of the ordinary given the constraints of the context. Compounding this, the development of smartphone and computer technology enables us to capture and send images easily, for free and instantly, and make and receive video calls across the world at the touch of a button through the device used to message them and without the need for special equipment. This makes it simple and seamless when it comes to sexual attraction, temptation, and decision-making in the heat-of-the-moment.

In Extract 32, Stuart broaches the topic of intimate messaging by couching it within a heavily hedged narrative that draws on the theme of coyness and tentative query. By drawing on his own embarrassment, Stuart attempts to present himself as a willing but cautious explorer of intimate messaging, driven by an underlying need for sharing 'emotionally and physically' (lines 1–2). Behaving in this way as a non-threatening but inquisitive actor, he lowers the perception of him as a risk if he is cautious too, and this is designed to invite a reciprocal response from the victim.

Extract 32

1.	Stuart:	There is so much I want to share with you – emotionally and
2.		physically. My thoughts are centered around you all the time and my
3.		body responds to these thoughts in a very good way. I should stop
4.		here at the risk of saying something too forward so i don't embarrass
5.		myself! How do you feel about sharing intimate types of thoughts? I
6.		don't mean crude or graphic things. Well, all I know is that it will be
7.		so nice to show you what I'm thinking when that day arrives.

He also hedges his request for intimate messaging in framing it as 'not crude or graphic' (line 6), but just 'what I'm thinking' (line 7) in advance of meeting. It is in this way that the intimate messaging is presented as non-threatening, the request as a hesitant and self-aware invitation, and the whole exercise as a pre-meeting discussion, which fixes the act of meeting as the ultimate goal. Built into this is the concept of sharing; a mutuality that defines the risk as joint and therefore mitigated. Subtle coercion disguised as flattery and the willingness to develop the relationship reinforces the activity as a seemingly mutually engaged, consensual endeavour.

The risks involved in sharing intimate moments online are mitigated by the context of a relationship, protected by the facade of trust and mutual sharing, as well as its appearance being limited to the two interacting individuals. It is not only enabled by the physical constraints of an online relationship but also by expectations of increasing intimacy in relationships as they develop; it is an explicit demonstration of trust. Therefore, not engaging in mutual intimate photo or video sharing can be weaponised by the fraudster as a sign of being non-committal to the relationship or a lack of trust in the other person, particularly when they appear to have sent images of themselves and expect reciprocation.

In another case, the fraudster has been sending unprompted explicit photos to the victim over the course of two weeks; however, during that time the victim has not reciprocated or made mention of the photos. We can see in Extract 33 that David's lack of engagement in relation to the photos is linked to his unease about the interaction and his suspicions that Penny is a fraudster. In this next exchange, the fraudster topicalises the photos with a narrative prior to sending them, in a move that suggests she is attempting to engage David in a discussion about her body.

This is mitigated through the narrative of embarrassment; she mentions being stared at by men, specifically mentioning her 'buttocks' (lines 4 and 6). However, together with intimate photos, and mentioning the shower and bath (lines 12 and 16), it is clear that the fraudster is using interactional techniques designed to conjure up images of the person in a nude or semi-nude state.

Extract 33

1.	Penny:	Hey love, how are you doing and how has your day been so far??
2.		Mine wasn't so good, some people got me upset today at the
3.		restaurant, they were gossiping about me as i walked in, they made
4.		my buttocks the topic of discussion, I felt so uncomfortable
5.	Penny:	The worst of it all is actually when i walk pass a guy, and he checks me
6.		out from head to toe, then turn around to checkout my buttocks, it's
7.		embarrassing
8.	Penny:	My Dad didn't leave a will, so the lawyer assisted me with the letter of
9.		the executorship from the high court
10.	Penny:	IMG.jpg (file attached)
11.	Penny:	IMG.jpg (file attached)
12.	Penny:	Anyways dear, i will go soak myself in a warm bath and see if i feel
13.		better afterwards,
14.	Penny:	IMG.jpg (file attached)
15.		Good Morning Love, how was your night? It's 8:20AM here now, just
16.		go out of the shower, thought I'd check on you, actually, I woke up
17.		this morning thinking of you, i think we have something good going
18.		between us, do you agree with me? I mean what other explanation do
19.		you call this when you go to bed at night and wake up the next
20.		morning, you think of same person?
21.	Penny:	IMG.jpg (file attached)
22.	David:	I appreciate all the pictures, but until we have spoken on a video call,
23.		it's quite hard for me to feel a strong level of commitment.

The response from David reflects his interpretation of the interaction and the explicit photos as an attempt by the sender to develop the relationship into one where they engage in reciprocal intimate messaging and photos of an intimate nature. Indeed, the modus operandi of sextortionists who operate on a non-relationship basis use reciprocity is a tool of gaining intimate images or messages from a victim (Tampubolon 2023).

In the following exchange, the fraudster (Matt) is attempting to engage the victim (Julie) in sexual discussions. It is clear that this is being driven by the fraudster by the way he manoeuvres the conversation towards sex on three occasions: on lines 4 and 7, and in his twisting of Julie's question about dancing (line 9) into one about sexual activity with her (line 10).

Extract 34
1. Matt: hello my love how are you sweetheart
2.   . . .
3. Matt   you are my everything that why i love you so much
4.   sex, knees [needs] or something else tell me please details
5.   we will do everything that couple does my love
6.   . . .
7. Matt   And yet, tell me what you like the most, so directly, I want to know please
8.   i like going out with my wife
9. Julie: do you like to dance?
10. Matt: hahaha yes my love dancing in bed will be whenever we want it but going
11.   out for party will be once in a while
12.   we go down sex slowly, you feel it in bed i will do it practical when i come
13.   haha

In Extract 35, Dan uses a series of tactics ranging from disguising the reality of the request through to more insistent demands in order to convince Peggy to send him intimate photos. In his opening attempt at eliciting an intimate picture, Dan uses the words 'nice pic' to mean an intimate photo. The use of 'nice' disguises the explicit nature of the request and mitigates its overt nature; however it is clear from Peggy's response, where she declines on account of not being comfortable with how she looks 'underneath [her clothes]' (lines 3 and 5), that she understands Dan's use of 'nice' as an encoded turn to mean naked.

Extract 35
1. Dan: You send me a nice pic pls
2. Peggy: Do I have too
3. Peggy: I am so not pretty underneath
4. Dan: Hun to my eyes you are xx
5. Peggy: Child birth and yoyo'ing weight have taken their toll
6. Dan: Don't care Hun send it
7. Peggy: I can't too embarrassed
8. Dan: Don't understand why you keep turning me down for what I love
9.   not nice
10. Peggy: [redacted image]

Following his initial flattery on line 4 to reassure Peggy he doesn't share her concerns about her body, Peggy's discomfort at servicing Dan's request is then met with a dismissive response 'Don't care' (line 6) when she continues to detail her concerns. After her outright rejection of his request on line 7, Dan responds with disappointment at Peggy 'turning me down' (line 8), and he details his apparent state of confusion to highlight the negative impact her rejection has had on him. This has echoes of domestic abuse in terms of the victim being made to feel they must act a certain way to appease their abuser. The impact this has on Peggy is clear as she moves from her position of rejection to agreeing to send an intimate photo in the next turn. The impact of his success in coercing the images from Peggy is seen in Extract 71, where only one month and eight days later, he weaponises them in order to extort money from her beyond her means.

Rejecting Requests from the Victim: To Meet in Person, Talk on the Phone or to Video Call

A key source of friction in the fraudster's journey of persuasion and manipulation is managing requests they cannot service, such as requests by the victim to meet them in person. These include victim requests for contact beyond the messaging already engaged in: video and phone calls, visits. These expectations arise in genuine online relationships but due to the nature of the fraud (the fraudster would become exposed or their story would start to unravel) need to be attended to in terms of denials and refusals from the fraudster, which are likely to cause the victim concerns about the legitimacy of the relationship.

The fraudster's performance here is based on receiving victim requests to meet and navigating the production of refusals while avoiding causing the victim alarm in doing so. This is done by continuing the context of the romance, using language of concern and frustration and the narrative of joint enterprise.

Rejecting Victim Requests to Meet

In Extract 36, James situates his excuse for not talking on the phone (urgent errands, line 5) at the end of a pre-account that reinforces the status of the relationship (lines 1–4); he uses the interactional space to reaffirm his feelings for her and to highlight the fact that they have mutual feelings.

Extract 36
1. James: How are you doing right now honey. It would have been a great
2.   pleasure to meet you as soon as I can especially with the way you
3.   have made me feel about and I like the fact that our feelings is
4.   mutual, but its so unfortunate that it won't be possible to meet with
5.   you due to an urgent errands I was explaining to you on the phone
6.   concerning my work and the project that was just approved.

We can see that he refers to them having spoken together on the phone (line 5), which mitigates concern that may arise from refusing to meet in person *and also* refuse other types of audio or visual contact. This also demonstrates his openness to explain multiple times, through multiple channels and apparent cooperation with the victim's wishes. The refusal itself, in a form of othering, is framed as an unfortunate impossibility despite his own willingness and eagerness to meet, due to a situation out of his control. That this is described as '*the* project that was *just approved*' (line 6, emphasis my own) draws attention to the fact that the project and its road to approval was something the victim had already been made aware of ('*the* project' rather than '*a* project'), and the use of '*just*' infers the immediacy of the information and the speed at which the fraudster is now having to act in order to service errands associated with this new-but-expected draw on his time.

Anticipating and matching victim frustration is also seen in the following series of extracts (Extracts 37–45), where the desire to meet is again articulated by the fraudster, but is escalated in this case by the fraudster (Camilla) having planned to take a chartered army plane to meet the victim (Roger) that day. The journey was never going to take place but the pretence did; the extracts that follow detail the conversations Camilla and Roger have while she is in the aeroplane hanger, ready to depart, and pretends to navigate impediments to that journey. In doing so she expresses repeated and increasing frustration at the plane being unable to take off, preventing her from flying to meet the victim (Roger) for the first time as she had planned and anticipated.

The visceral responses of the fraudster, shown through her displays of mental and physical distress at the ongoing delays to the flight that was supposed to get her to Roger that day, serve to implicitly reinforce these delays as unwanted, unexpected, and the result of a situation outside of her control. This also deflects attention away from her and the credibility of the situation. It is also a jointly experienced frustration (with Camilla bearing the brunt of this), and as such, she is positioned beyond reproach for the unfortunate situation.

Extract 37
11.   I've had no meals yet babe . . . . couldn't be bothered really x x x ♥♥♥

Extract 38
68.   Camilla: Babes it was the worst sleeping condition ever love
69.   x x x x I swear x x x xx

Amidst this, she also focuses on Roger, showing herself to be selfless and concerned about him when she is the one that is in discomfort.

Extract 39
1.   Camilla: You alright ? Z x x did you sleep at all ? As you could guess . . . hardly
2.   got some good sleep really. ♥♥♥♥

Camilla then escalates the outward manifestation of her distress. Increasing her visceral response to the situation to a point of extreme ('I might grab someone's gun and just shoot', line 72) shows how she maintains tension throughout a protracted period, increasing the tension as time passes. This manifestation of trauma bombing manifests as a type of reverse love bombing, where instead of increasing proclamations of love in implicit and explicit ways following concerning behaviour by the fraudster, the fraudster *increases their distress*. This serves manifold purposes: the distress of the fraudster distracts the victim from examining the reasons behind a new concerning situation; it draws a protective response from the victim where they will attempt to relieve the distress of the fraudster; and the victim will dampen their own emotional response to the situation in order to avoid increasing the already heightened distress of the fraudster.

Extract 40

70.	Camilla :	Your girl' tired and angry babe x x xx.
71.		We still haven't moved x x xx bloody hell x x x x
72.		Now I'm thinking I might grab someone's gun and just shoot x
73.		x x x x

Extract 41

| 165. | Camilla: | Babes I'm sad and down . . .. I've never felt this low since the |
| 166. | | worst days of my life babe x x x x x |

As Extracts 42–45 show, this encourages reciprocal care, and also serves to dampen Roger's visceral responses to the situation (Extract 44), tempering his own frustration, encouraging him to draw his energies towards protecting and assisting Camilla (Extracts 42 and 43), and demonstrates the success of Camilla's deflection of blame onto other parties (Extract 45).

Extract 42

| 24. | Roger: | I'm frustrated by it, so god knows how you must be feeling XxX |
| 25. | | ♡⊘♡⊘♡ |

Extract 43

| 46. | Roger: | You must be bush whacked babes – all this waiting around you've had |
| 47. | | to do – you're the one that matters here XxX |

Extract 44

127.	Roger:	Well, too say I'm not happy about that is an understatement
128.		XxX Don't know what too say to be honest ♡⊘♡⊘♡
129.		No point me being – it'll get me nowhere XxX
130.		I can only imagine how your feeling if I'm feeling the way I am

Extract 45

| 153. | Roger: | Everything's out of my hands Beautiful- I'm relying on other peeps |
| 154. | | too get you home and they've all failed me right now XxX |

Rejecting Victim Requests to Video or Phone Chat: Deflecting by Accusing Victim

Other types of requests from the victim that the fraudster may not be able to service are meeting in an online video chat or talking on the phone. Both of these, in the absence of being able to meet in person, are legitimate alternative communication options available to individuals in online or long-distance relationships, in order for both parties to see and/or speak to each other. Much like discussed earlier in relation to meeting in person, this is something that fraudsters often avoid as it could expose their real identity as visually or orally incompatible with the identity of the person they claim to be. Excuses to not meet via video or over the phone are given as a 'red flag' in public protect literature (for example, CrimeStoppers 2023), so this element of the interaction is a particular touchpoint where their illegitimacy could potentially be exposed. Refusals to engage online and/or over the phone could reasonably cause the victim concern, more so than refusals to meet in person, as many fraudsters use the physical distance between them and the difficulties meeting as part of the fraud itself (for example, asking for money so they can afford to fly to the victim and set up a life with them, Extract 55). Online and telephone interactions are so commonplace and easily accessible, all the more so since the Covid-19 pandemic, on a multitude of video-conferencing apps, rather than difficult or unusual types of communication requiring special technology. The ease in online communications beyond the textual is particularly the case when we consider that many romance frauds are conducted through Wi-Fi-based communication apps such as WhatsApp, which have an inbuilt function specifically for easy and accessible video and audio call capabilities.

The refusal of a partner's ostensibly benign, uncomplicated and, given the context of an online relationship, entirely expected request such as an invitation to talk via video or phone call is a difficult prospect for fraudsters. In denying this type of contact they risk damage to the facade of reassurance that is so essential in building and maintaining rapport and creating common interactional ground based on love and romance. This leaves what is termed here as a '*reassurance void*' through which the victim may begin to question the legitimacy of the relationship and expose its reality. To counteract this, the fraudster will need to provide a convincing reason why they are unable to agree to this request and, optimally, quash future requests in the process. More than this, they will need to align this reason within the wider context of the relationship that has been developed thus far so as to not compromise it by behaving in a way that could cause the victim concern.

Extracts 46–48 show how the inversion of trust as a reality and expectation is performed by the fraudster through their response of being affronted and disappointed by the victim's requests to meet online or in person. The fraudster in Extract 46 responds to the victim's request that they communicate via video by implying it's not him that is preventing this, or a lack of willing on his part; there is a practical barrier to this happening (his captain needs to authorise this and there is a process involved in order for that to happen). The fraudster also attends to the act of her asking this by reframing it as an indication that she doesn't trust him and is acting in a way that is going against the relationship, and him.

Extract 46
1. F: Well baby, I have to apply to my captain. I hope he gives me access to the
2.   call. You shouldn't feel like this. Am your man. except you don't trust me,
3.   you shouldn't feel that way. Am your man but you don't trust me.

He repeats 'am your man' and 'you don't trust me' twice on lines 2 and 3, posing them as opposing statements through the use of 'except' (line 2) and 'but' (line 3) in a comparative construction that places a negative as the counterpart to the first element. Here the fraudster is using trust as a way to steer the victim's behaviour, using it as a tool through which to combat the very act of her questioning him and also the relationship. This serves to redirect the conversation towards broader questions around the relationship, distracting the victim into defending their trustworthiness and why they are requesting a video chat, and away from the issue of the chat and why the fraudster is refusing.

Victim Challenges of Fraudster Refusals

During an interaction with a fraudster, the victim may raise concerns at various points, such as at the point when the fraudster refuses to meet in person or online, or when information doesn't match the conversation.

In Extract 47, the victim is attempting to enact self-protective mechanisms in the form of asking that they meet before she can fully commit to and trust the relationship. The fraudster uses the victim's attempt at self-protection against her by turning her request to meet him into a reflection of her own lack of trustworthiness. It is in this way that victim efforts to protect are transformed and distorted, and future attempts are dissuaded.

Extract 47
1. F: I am always goin to be with you and I want you to get that in your head
2. V: Thank you. It's there. We just have to cement it by meeting.
3. F: That's very important but if we do not trust each other how can we do that
4. F: And how can I trust you then you don't trust me

Extract 48 is from a fraudster who is responding to the victim questioning his intentions because he will not communicate via video or provide his address in order for her to verify his identity. The fraudster first responds with annoyance that she still persists on pursuing a video call after he has done everything else that was asked of him (to prove himself legitimate), and then makes clear his broader misogynistic issue with her continued requests for a video call (lines 1–2), attempting to nullify her right to request any evidence of his authenticity on the basis of her gender. He takes the request that she makes in order to satisfy her concerns and fears about the relationship (as she later states, 'please give me what I need to be safe', and harnesses it as a way to redirect the blame onto her for not being trusting and to show his disappointment in her behaviour.

Extract 48
1. F: I've done it all, I'm a man and you're a woman, you shouldn't be the
2.   one who commands me no matter what, though I respect you
3.   enough.
4. V: women have the same rights here as men, I don't command I want
5.   evidence, if you love me then you understand where is the video
6. F: your act here doesn't show there is love any more but as a man i will
7.   Endure what ever come out from you, what i am seeing here
8.   can never come between two lovers i am very disappointed

In Extract 49, the victim (Lily) has become frustrated at the fraudster's (James B) repeated excuses in relation to talking on the phone or meeting her, which results in the following interaction. Lily directly addresses the issue on line 2, using 'actually' and 'basics' to convey her incredulity at having to reiterate her as yet unfulfilled request, despite its simple nature (as opposed to the fraudster's offerings of buying her a house) and its position as a rudimentary part of a relationship. Clift (2001) describes this use of 'actually' as a 'counterinforming' word used to introduce 'disjunctive material' as rare, and if it is used it will be highly mitigated, for example with the use of 'well' to signal the dispreferred nature of the turn (Heritage 1984). The victim's use of 'actually' without any mitigating language to soften its impact, indeed her use of 'basics' (line 2) at the end of this turn intensifies and further demonstrates her frustration with the fraudster and his repeated refusals to talk on the phone or meet in person.

Extract 49
1. James B: What did you want me to do for you then
2. Lily: Actually meet me speak to me on the phone basics
3. Lily: I never asked you to buy a house i never asked for money
4. James B: We got to have a family planning please
5. James B: I need us to leave on [live in] our own house please
6. James B: Stop making it difficult to me.

This interpretation is supported in the following turn, on line 3, where we see Lily contrasting the inability of the fraudster to commit to talking on the phone with his ability to actively perform other acts and pursue other topics: raising money to buy a house together and offering her a return on the money she has and will be giving him. James B's response in line 6 frames Lily's statements as a source of difficulty for him rather than a legitimate concern, and therefore as something she needs to stop doing rather than something that needs addressing. It is within this context that James B avoids addressing the issue of contact she had raised. He also presents a contrasting imploring response in relation to Lily's more direct, aggressive turn through the use of 'please' (lines 4 and 5) in an act alike to pleading with Lily to continue to plan for their future family and to direct funds towards this joint ('we', 'us', 'our') aim; couching this within a needs-based framework ('got to', 'I need').

The fraudster in Extract 50, Irene, addresses the victim (Robert's) request through developing a narrative of self-protection and caution around the speed of the relationship (video-chatting represents the relationship moving 'too fast', lines 18–19), rationalised by a previous negative relationship experience. We can see this through the shift in interpretation of Irene's rejection in Extract 50: first as caution stemming from her not knowing much about him ('ask away') and her status as a non-native English speaker (lines 3 and 4), and then as concern about getting close in that way to a man 'I am . . . a nice guy' (line 20).

Extract 50

1.	Robert:	Do you fancy speaking now?
2.	Irene:	I think we need to know more
3.	Robert:	As I say.. ask away.. you are quite cautious? I understand English is
4.		not your first language. It's not a problem. ☺
5.	Irene:	Yeah, I'm a little cautious. My last relationship hurt me a lot
6.	Robert:	Sorry to hear that. Was it recently? I know its hard, but you have to
7.		try and "love like you have never been hurt".
8.	Irene:	No, two years ago, I was just coming out of a relationship that hurtme
9.	Robert:	Ok.. To me, chatting on video is not committing to anything. Its just
10.		the equivalent of meeting someone casually at a party, or down the
11.		gym.
12.	Irene:	I think if we make a video, it means that we have confirmed the
13.		relationship, what do you think
14.	Robert:	I would very much disagree. Sorry.. If you think that way, I am not
15.		surprised you are cautious. It's just part of getting to know someone.
16.		You don't really know too much from a few messages. You can
17.		exchange a lot of information very quickly in a video chat.
18.	Irene:	I hope you can give me a little more time, okay? I don't want to go too
19.		fast
20.		Robert: Thats ok. ☺. I am quite a nice guy, but I suppose they all say
21.		that! 😁

Through this dialogue, Irene weaves Robert's request to video chat into an advance that oversteps the current boundaries of the relationship (line 5), something not shared by Robert (lines 9–11). These narratives around feeling vulnerable and protecting herself are encoded in some gender-normative dynamics around vulnerability and power, enabling Irene to directly refuse the victim's request to chat via video and also deny him recourse.

Through this lens Irene responds to his request with a request of her own, for more time before agreeing to video chat (line 18). It is in this way that Irene does not need to produce different responses or mitigations for future requests throughout the relationship. Her sense of personal comfort and safety, and her feeling of security in the relationship, is what is preventing her from chatting via video with Robert; this could wax and wane, and is not bound by any particular timescale. This mitigation is useful conceptually because if Robert pushes Irene on the matter, she will then likely feel more anxious in the relationship and less likely to want to video chat. Robert is in the position where he had not known the link between adding communication channels and an increase in relationship status (lines 13–14). He is now incentivised to make Irene as happy as possible in order to gain the trust and level of comfort she requires to video chat, which to her signifies the next step in the relationship (line 12–13). Indeed, several turns later, Irene intimates that the relationship may not continue, but would be willing to meet if they are still together romantically: 'It depends on the relationship between us. When we are together, I hope to see you soon' (Irene). This appears to be an unusual stance as there has been no talk of this up to this point. As such, this suggests the relationship is waning or that its immediate future is in question; therefore, both serve as a warning to Robert against actions that could negatively affect the relationship further, and also reveal an exit strategy for Irene from having to actually service video and physical meetings in the future.

Shortly after this, in Extract 51, Irene uses her rejection of Robert's offer to video chat to steer the conversation towards monetisation, with her investments keeping her too busy to video chat (lines 3–4). Robert querying Irene's commitment to the relationship (lines 5–6) leads her to state in her next turn that spending time and being successful in this specific cryptocurrency investment will enable her to be 'more serious' (lines 7–8) in the relationship; she represents her time spent investing in cryptocurrencies as an act that is beneficial for their relationship. This is an important counterpoint to and panacea for her earlier uncertainty about its longevity and also serves to mitigate her further refusal (unavailability) to video chat, reframing it as an act that will benefit them both. Indirectly, specifying the anticipated fruits of her labours also acts to incentive Robert to explore cryptocurrencies himself to experience a level of success that could mean enough money to 'buy a house and a car' (line 7) through one investment.

Extract 51

166.	Robert:	No time for a quick video chat? Friday morning
167.		maybe?
168.	Irene:	Yes, I will be busy
169.	Irene:	I need to look at the cryptocurrency I'm investing in
170.	Robert:	You don't seem very keen to move things on … ? I am not a
171.		priority … ? No worries. 😀
172.	Irene:	No, I hope to be able to buy a house and a car through this
173.		investment, so I will be more serious

This final extract of this section shows the topic of investment being introduced into the developing romantic relationship. In the following section we will explore in detail how fraudsters introduce requests for money within the framework they have built, established, and then need to maintain as a legitimate and ongoing romantic relationship.

Finance

Requests for money in romance fraud are rarely 'one-off', as the modus operandi of this crime is gaining money through deception over an extended period of time, where requests will be repeated until the relationship breaks down. This section explores the ways that successful requests for money manifest in romance frauds, and what tactics fraudsters use to mitigate the concern that is likely to accompany such a request. It reveals that drawing on joint responsibility, the principal of reciprocity, and visceral responses are present in direct appeals for money, while distancing and displaying vulnerabilities are used to reframe and mitigate such requests.

Reframings and Mitigations

In Extract 52, the fraudster (Adam) is asking the victim (Carly) for money. He opens this sequence by stating there is 'nothing to write about' (line 1), downplaying and contradicting the soon-to-be-revealed emotional and financial predicament that this statement precedes. He continues by referring to himself in the third person (line 1), which, together with his profession ('engineer') and temporary nature of his predicament (line 2), distances himself from his talk of him looking or feeling incompetent (line 3). He follows this with more distancing, with the use of the idiom 'in the mud' (lines 1–2) instead of directly saying he is in trouble, and the use of laughing emojis, at odds with the lexical content, to indicate him laughing it off or laughing at his own predicament, perhaps as a display of vulnerability or embarrassment. This is supported by Adam's use of a crying emoji on line 3, which is a semiotic representation of sadness he feels from being made to look in some way incompetent (line 3). Fraudsters showing vulnerability and producing visceral responses that show their physical or emotional anguish is a way in which they can draw a protective response from the victim (Carter 2021). This is made more acute and powerful when the display of vulnerability appears to be uneasy or unwilling.

Extract 52

1.	Adam:	As for me there's nothing to write about . Engineer Adam is in the
2.		mud 😂😂 I don't like what's going on at the moment and
3.		this is giving me shades of incompetence 😨 I tried applying for a
4.		loan here but I was denied because I don't have a business here in
5.		Turkey. But I've been able to raise $9 k so far. I need assistance 😂 if
6.		you can loan me It doesn't matter the interest you'll get it as soon as I
7.		get back 🙈 I will have another problem if I don't return by
8.		tomorrow. I've ran out of time

Adam then follows this with pre-financial-request mitigations in the form of first detailing his efforts to help himself, which frames his request-to-come as not the sole burden of the victim, and as a final resort after his attempts to help himself; he has attempted to get more funds through a loan (lines 4–5), has raised some of the money himself (line 5) and is continuing to raise more (implied in his use of 'so far'). Asking for money to add to money that they have already contributed is a tactic in romance fraud as it lessens the sense of risk for the victim, as they are not being asked to pay the entire amount, and also the risk seems shared, which lessens the risk in practical terms but also implies that the other person has deemed providing money themselves as safe (Carter 2021). Adam makes clear that Carly's money is a temporary loan that will be returned to her with interest; how much extra this will be 'doesn't matter' (line 6), suggesting that money is not usually an issue for Adam and won't be shortly.

The request for money from the victim is also minimised as 'assistance' (line 5) and as a 'loan' (line 6); the mirroring of the attempt to get a business loan (lines 4–5) and then asking the victim for a loan (line 6) reinforces the legitimacy of the request as she is not the first place he went to for money. The use of the laughing emoji on line 5 again serves to downplay the need for assistance and, in the absence of genuinely amusing talk, together with an emoji of a monkey covering its eyes, appears to convey his embarrassment and vulnerability in relation to his predicament.

Adam conveys urgency in a direct way by telling Carly that he has run out of time (line 8), and unless he gets the rest of the money, there will be further problems. This statement of urgency relies on the (fictional) pressure from an external source to drive the fraudster's request; it is framed as his hand being forced by this external factor rather than the request coming directly from him and motivated by a personal need, for example to buy luxury items.

Requests for money are also more explicitly reframed in order to disguise the risks, concerns, and reality of what the fraudster is asking of the victim, shown in Extract 53 by the fraudster foregrounding the singular (return and increase on their 'investment', gifts, and his physical presence) and joint (contribution to the relationship, part of a shared enterprise, for a shared outcome) incentives of sending money.

Extract 53
1.   F: I am very grateful for your help so far and must pay you back even with
2.   interest.I shouldn't be that ungrateful not to surprise you with marvel at as
3.   my beloved.I have something special for you as we finish with this and I
4.   coming to meet you over there in your country

The use of 'even' (line 1) signifies the representation of the giving of money not as a loan (which would be expected to be paid back with interest) but as something that will be treated as such in terms of a beneficial monetary outcome for the victim. This acts as an incentive for the victim to agree to lend the fraudster the money. It provides a familiar context through which that money lending occurs; it legitimises the act, while the unneeded offering of additional money to the victim provides a facade of credibility to the fraudster in terms of generosity, fairness, and access to sums of money.

James' turn in Extract 54, with its use of 'then', situates his half of the payment as contingent on the victim paying hers, and the use of 'remember' draws on a previously agreed state, which keeps the victim accountable and underpins the request. Other ways this is performed is through the 'set-up' (Carter 2021), where more abstract agreements around behaviours are established and then later used by the fraudster to compel actions based on these. Here, the use of 'remember' is more explicit, and is used to ensure the victim complies with actions they have previously agreed to.

Extract 54
      James B: Remember you said you gon get £120.000 babe then I can equal get mine

This also presents the victim's money as part of an equal burden for both partners in the relationship, equal risk, and therefore reducing concerns that may be born from the victim feeling as though they are the sole bearer of providing the 'full amount' needed.

In Extract 55, Graham draws on three elements to incentivise and compel the victim to give him her money: a visceral response (current concern and worry over his future life direction); framing the money as something that they both need rather than it being a unidirectional giving of money to him; and to make them meeting in person a reality quicker.

Extract 55

> Graham: I'm worried and don't know where my life is heading now darling.. We need to get this 3 k to sort things out so I can fly in your arms quickly

These elements reduce the perception of risk, framing it as a joint project for a mutually beneficial outcome. Drawing on this, requests for money are also situated within the normalised expectations between a husband and wife. The messages in Extract 56 from the fraudster (Avery) draw on a risk-reduction, incentive-based approach, where Mandy's (the victim's) money will leave her account for a short time before being repaid, and repaid with interest (lines 3 and 4), before leveraging his (false) position as her husband and the increased responsibility spouses have for each other's wellbeing, financial or otherwise.

Extract 56

1.	Avery:	Darling you know I have workers who are working for me at the club
2.		but I have to pay so that the good can be clear darling kindly give me
3.		the money and I will pay it in a few weeks and even add interest for
4.		you
5.	Avery:	Do you best for your husband
6.	Avery:	I will add more to it few weeks

Topicalising their (fictitious) marital status in this part of the interaction is suggestive of another type of incentivisation: the fraudster is implying their relationship is at the level of trust and commitment of a married couple, and suggests marriage could be on the horizon (something that the victim does want to happen). He then returns to explicit incentivisation on line 6 with 'I will add more to it few weeks', moving reimbursement beyond interest, with its fixed rates, to a more casual 'adding' of money, again within a relatively short timeframe.

Visceral Responses and Pressure

In Extract 57, the fraudster (Ben) frames the request for money as a final request of Amy (the victim). He uses the phrase 'this last time' on line 3, which evokes a finality of this payment, a last hurdle to overcome before the relationship can continue without difficulty, and she will shortly see the return of her money. This tactic encourages victims to continue, providing motivation and incentive even if they have doubts about the person they are in a relationship with. This is because the act of giving money then becomes finite and, as seen in sunk cost fallacy, to stop prior to this would mean the financial and emotional investment of the victim's past efforts, in terms of money sent to the fraudster and past and continued beliefs in their credibility, would be wasted, and the victim would have to face a devastating truth.

Extract 57
1. Ben: My Angel,I really do not know what to do at the moment because I haven't
2.   still completed the money yet.Please,I will pay you all the money back but for
3.   this last time do something for us sweetheart . . .

Prior to this, Ben projects a sense of panic on line 1, which can draw a protective response from victims (Carter 2021); he also uses 'at the moment' and 'yet', which offer a sense of temporality, bringing the issue to the immediate present and encouraging a rapid response (Carter 2023). He then follows this with a statement that acknowledges there have been other payments by Amy to him '*all* the money' (line 2), which he will return. Crucially, this is tempered with the use of 'but' (line 2), which acts as a condition of return; Amy must first perform another act. This act is not made explicit; it is euphemistically referred to as 'something for us' (line 3) which achieves two ends: it enables Ben to avoid specifically mentioning money again and drawing attention to what is another financial request, as well as reframing the act as not another one-way transfer of money from Amy to him but as something that benefits the both of them. Ben's turn is bookended by terms of endearment 'My Angel' (line 1) and 'sweetheart' (line 3), which perform a type of love bombing, particularly prevalent in interactions where the perpetrator's requests or behaviours may cause concern or alarm to the recipient. In this case, as in many, this takes the form of another request for money.

In Extract 58, the fraudster (D) uses visceral responses to present his request for money as a desperate need, brought about by medical necessity and hastened by the physical pain he claims to be experiencing, which is causing severe psychological harm. The use of the word 'this' in the fraudster's turn 'If I had this 3 k' (line 2) orients the victim to a specific 3 k that needs to be obtained, from her, personalising it as her problem and isolating her as the source of the money. This increases the pressure on the victim to comply quickly, and to avoid the possible harm to his life described in his following turns.

Extract 58
1. D: It is killing me slowly darling
2. D: If I had this 3 k, I would have replaced it and solved this issue .
3. D: I don't know what to do
4. D: Feel like killing myself darling
5. D: Because I don't know why I'm always coming up obstacles that's more over
6.   than me
7. B: Please don't talk like that, I'm trying my hardest to get the 3 k back
8. D: I'm aware of everything darling .

9.	D:	I'm talking about buying this prescribed drug to reduce the deep pains I'm
10.		going through darling
11.	B:	I know
12.	D:	That's the reason why I feel like killing myself because the pains I'm going
13.		through is extraordinary
14.	B:	I understand,, but I haven't got that much

The fraudster is claiming that he would have 'solved this issue' (line 2) himself if he had the means, but as he hasn't, the desperation and life-threatening nature of the situation demands that he ask others for help. This is a type of othering that relies on the situation to apply the pressure rather than the individual's whim; othering is also seen in the use of 'issue' (line 2) and 'obstacles' (line 5) which serves to distance the fraudster from the specifics of the situation that this money is required to resolve. The vagueness also allows the 'situation' to remain wider and ongoing, and potentially the source of further, repeat requests for money, and closes off opportunities for the victim to interrogate the situation for discrepancies or concerns.

In the first line of Extract 59, the fraudster describes himself as 'good. Just lil upset' (line 1). Although most of the victim responses have been redacted from this exchange (at the victim's request), it is clear that the fraudster is using an extreme visceral response, a threat to life, in response to his (fictitious) difficult situation, a jarring counterpart to his prior turn. This is used to compel a protective response from the victim, which he compounds by explicitly directing the victim to 'assist' him (line 5) after telling her he is suicidal at that very moment.

Extract 59

1.	F:	Am good. Just lil upset
2.	F:	My friend had an accident with my new car that is not up to a week
3.	F:	I feel like committing suicide rite now baby
4.	V:	Ooyy, sorry about that baby. You don't want me to come see you baby?
5.	F:	You have to assist me on funding to add to what I have so as to make it
6.		happen
7.	F:	I know that baby, I never ask for much is just to support what I have so as to
8.		make it
9.	F:	From $500 to $800, any amount you can help me with
10.	F:	This is you and I
11.		How much do you have to support me?

Following the victim's offer to come and see him, in his next turn he then mitigates the criticality of his request by recategorising it as 'support' (line 7 and, later still, something to 'help me with' on line 9). This is further tempered through his use of 'just', which directs the victim away from immediate physical assistance and acts as a way to highlight that the route to help him is through money, and serves to minimise the subsequent financial disruption to the victim (Carter 2023). He then continues by further reducing the burden on the victim by describing his financial need as 'any amount' (line 9), depending on what she can offer him (line 11) and something to add to/support what he has raised already (lines 5 and 7), suggesting that he is not entirely reliant on the victim, and that she has some agency in this.

Navigating Victim Refusals and Direct Challenges

But what happens when requests or demands for money are refused or rejected by the victim? Earlier we explored how *fraudsters* reject requests that they cannot service while maintaining the romantic facade; in this section we see *victims* rejecting the fraudsters' requests for money, and responses by fraudsters to victims who have challenged their authenticity and credibility. Refusals from the victim can occur for a variety of reasons: Extracts 60–65 are cases where the victim has refused to continue sending the fraudster money. It is in these interactions we see the fraudster increasing in aggression and escalating the relationship status in their attempts to convince the victim otherwise.

The following exchange occurs when the victim does not want to give the fraudster any more money. The premise of needing money is predicated on a 'deal' the fraudster needs to do. In Extract 60, the fraudster leverages the narrative that the victim has not only joint responsibility for their success (encapsulated in her use of 'our', 'we', and 'us' throughout), but also singles the victim out as solely responsible if 'the deal' fails. Money is at first referred to as supporting her (line 2) and 'all we need to succeed' (line 4). At the request of the victim, their responses have been removed from the extract; however, it is clear that the victim does not agree to send the money, as the fraudster's responses throughout Extract 60 become shorter and more direct, and repetitive (with the final three turns close repeats of 'borrow the money', lines 6, 7, and 8).

Extract 60
1. F: If will fail in this deal, I will hold you responsible for our failure, because I
2.   tried all my effort to succeed, but you have not supported me. My dear
3.   please try all you could to sell some of your properties and get the money,
4.   that's all we need to succeed don't disappoint me I have so much confidence
5.   in you and I believe you can do it
6. F: Try to borrow money [angry face]
7. F: Borrow the money
8. F: Borrow the money for us to succeed

The fraudster uses both emotional incentives and threats in her attempt to coerce the victim into giving her money. She repeatedly frames the victim giving money as allowing her or them to 'succeed', and she has the confidence and belief in him to do so (lines 2, 4, and 5) while also threatening him with being responsible for the failure, and for disappointing her if he doesn't. She offers practical advice on how to raise the funds needed, suggesting that the victim doesn't have the money that is being asked of him. By referring to his properties in the plural, the fraudster leverages knowledge about the victim that she has gleaned through their relationship so far, demonstrating how information can be weaponised and also laying bare that fraudsters don't stop when victims have run out of money.

If we now look at what happens when a victim withdraws from the relationship after the fraudster asks him for money, in Extract 61 David first summarises his concerns, including the fraudster's refusals to video chat and mention of investments (as seen in Extracts 50 and 51) which have led him to refuse to give Penny the £750 she had requested. Penny's response is one of anger, describing David's conclusions about her as being spoken down to (line 5), an insult (lines 9, 12, and 14), and disappointment (line 15). The fraudster's 'if I had known' (lines 6 and 14) imply the victim has let the fraudster down and not lived up to their expectations of a romantic partner; therefore, it has been a waste of time getting to know the victim.

Extract 61

1.	David:	given the seductive pics, the hard-luck stories (to encourage
2.		sympathy), lack of a video chat, and now the request for money, you
3.		have the profile of a Catfish.
4.	Penny:	Catfish? today must be the worst day of my life, i have never
5.		been talk down like this ever, i didn't know asking you for help would
6.		cost me so much, if i had known, I wouldn't have bothered
7.	Penny:	Yes you hinted on not committing until we've had a video
8.		conversation, of which i never refused, just that i haven't been able to
9.		make calls since i got to Cape Town, and you just insulted my effort
10.		and openness to you, all the talk about my Dad's estate and the pics
11.		was out of my freewill, to communicate and get to know each other,
12.		and you just insulted all that
13.	Penny:	You know what, i asked for a loan, which i was going to pay back, i
14.		didn't ask for insults, and if i had known you would react this way,
15.		i would not have asked you for help, i never expected this from you

Penny reframes her actions that have caused David the most concern (listed on lines 1 and 2) as immediate and temporary difficulties due to her location (video call refusals), examples of her openness and honesty (talk of her dad's estate), and as efforts to communicate and develop the relationship (intimate photos). His concerns about Penny's legitimacy had been building over time; all of the elements here could be accepted. However, it is the ask for money that caused David to question the legitimacy of the relationship; indeed, after her request he tells her 'I was expecting a request for money.' Shortly after this exchange, David ended the relationship by ceasing communication and blocking Penny's number.

Extract 62 shows the victim questioning the fraudster's repeated requests for money. By elevating the victim's role from girlfriend to wife, the fraudster defends and explains his requests for money by harnessing the normative expectations of married partners to share finances and assist each other. He also leverages her role as wife to portray her as his only available source of assistance and narrowing his options of help to her exclusively, based on the flattering, but in reality isolating, claim that she is the only person he trusts.

Extract 62
1. V: So why are you always asking me for money?
2. F: You are my wife and you are the only one [finger emoji] I trust with my life
3.   and the kids life.!

He emphasises this by referring to his life and the lives of his children, invoking a sense of duty and responsibility as wife and mother that is very specific to that one person. Similarities lie here with coercive control, where perpetrators narrow the victim's world to create a feeling of responsibility for the abuser and their wellbeing; this is a duty that cannot be shared with others and is therefore a tool of isolation.

The use of role escalation from online dating partner to wife and mother is a common tactic, despite the improbability of either or both of these states occurring in a relationship between two parties that are yet to meet in person. However, in Extract 63, the fraudster (Bill) uses this escalation to directly attack the victim after she challenges his motives for asking her for money and questions what he really needs it for.

Extract 63
1. Bill: DO you think I'm lying to you my wife the mother of my kids? You are the
2.   mother of my kids and
3. Bill: Why are you making me to feel all this pains
4. Bill: Why are you doing this to my heart?
5. Bill: You think I'm after your money? You think I'm lying to you about my
6.   retirement money?

He issues a series of questions which give the impression of an aggressive and accusatory response, directed towards twisting the victim's querying of his veracity as an act of harm against him. This shows the fraudster escalating not only the roles within the relationship as a tool through which he can increase the power of his response (drawing on the normative values of husband and wife and the increased expectations of truthfulness from pre to post-wedding vows), but also Bill substantially increasing his emotional real estate. He takes the victim's question in relation to his truthfulness and overpowers it with an emotionally charged visceral response that then switches the accusation from him and onto the victim for causing him pain.

The interaction in Extract 64 shows the fraudster's distortion of the abuser–victim paradigm, in which James B, when outed as a fraudster by Lily, produces responses that claim emotional trauma as a result of her actions. This type of emotional manipulation relies on visceral responses and redirects Lily's legitimate claim to victimhood, claiming it for his own.

Extract 64

1.	Lily:	I want my money back
2.	James B:	Just leave me alone I wanna be left alone now
3.	James B:	Don't talk to me anymore
4.	James B:	I told you I have depressed for years now
5.	Lily:	Join the club
6.	James B:	You're not helping at all thanks I'm gone
7.	Lily:	Thank your mum and lawyer for breaking us up
8.	Lily:	And yourself
9.	James B:	I'm going to kill myself now
10.	James B:	I'll miss you so much
11.	James B:	So you won't have to hear from me anymore
12.	James B:	Bye. Babe

Through this interaction we can see the layers of responsibility placed on Lily by James B, and the control he attempts to exert through this; she is required to not contact him unless he wants to be contacted (lines 2 and 3), she is expected to be careful in her communications to not exacerbate (implicit, line 4) and also help heal his depression (line 6). When she does not attend to his claim to mental health difficulties, and instead nullifies them with her own counter-claim for the same difficulties (line 5), he explicitly accuses her of 'not helping' (line 6) and escalates his claim to threatening to leave the relationship ('I'm gone') and more extreme psychological trauma in claiming he is suicidal. He frames her as responsible for his decision to end his own life (lines 9 and 11), which he will do despite his feelings for her which are delivered here in contrast to his narrative of her failing him (lines 10 and 12) and of him feeling that he is a burden to her ('so you won't have to hear from me anymore', line 11).

Turning a victim's demand for their money back against the victim and using emotional escalation in response to make them feel they are doing something wrong, hurtful, or damaging, and the threat to life 'I'm going to kill myself now' (line 9) are also tactics commonly seen in other types of abusive relationship such as in those involving coercive control and domestic violence and abuse (Fitzpatrick et al. 2022).

This same passive aggressive response type is also present in Extract 65, delivered through the discord arising from Stuart's dissatisfaction at the victim's refusal to send him money. His well-prefaced turn on line 1 signals dissatisfaction with the victim's prior turn (Pomerantz and Heritage 2013) in which she refuses his request. This is topicalised through his characterisation of her refusal as 'running away' from him, which is contrasted with his apparent gratitude ('thank you', line 1) and sign-off ('have a wonderful day', line 3) to deliver a passively hostile turn.

Extract 65
1.   Stuart: well thank you for running way from me. i want you to remember
2.   your promise that you will always be there when i need your help may
3.   you have a wonderful day"

The fraudster explicitly orients back to his earlier interaction with the victim in Extract 10 where Stuart delivers his belief that they will 'always be there for each other'; he uses this to passively accuse the victim of failing to meet her promises to him. This demonstrates how the early interaction during the opening, rapport building, and scripting stages of the relationship are used for purposes beyond these tasks; they are used to elicit 'promises' and behavioural ideals from the victim that will then later be used to coerce the victim into acting.

Post-romance

Ending the fraudulent relationship does not necessarily signal freedom for the victim from the fraudster's communications or the end of the financial abuse. These final extracts show interactions from romance frauds where the fraudster pivots their criminality into sextortion and threat, weaponising context they have drawn from the victim during the 'relationship'.

In the following interaction the fraudster has moved into issuing direct threats, which centre around trying to get the victim to respond; prior to this, the victim had refused to give the fraudster any more money and had stopped replying to his messages. The move into threat mirrors the escalation often seen in domestic violence and abuse when the perpetrator senses they have lost control of the victim or they are going to leave the relationship (Campbell et al. 2003).

Extract 66
1.   F: Am really not happy
2.   F: About how.You are treating me

3. F: You are very very stupid
4. F: You know
5. F: Because of this your act
6. F: Look and going to make you suffer
7. F: And waste Your life in jail
8. F: What [watch] out
9. F: Then
10. F: If you don't reply to Me.
11. F: You will see what I. will do

The fraudster first articulates the impact of the victim's behaviour (refusing to send him money) on his emotional state (lines 1 and 2) before directly insulting her (line 3), and making explicit there will be consequences of her actions ('because of this your act', line 5). These consequences are jail for an unspecified reason (line 7), in addition to the more abstract threats ('going to make you suffer', line 6; 'you will see what I will do', line 11). The fraudster makes clear that his negative emotional state and the actions he will take in relation to this are the result of her actions, a typical response in domestic abuse. The physical delivery of these messages compound the harm, sent as they were in quick succession, causing the victim's phone to be inundated with multiple messages, which can cause stress to the recipient (Thomee et al. 2007).

Placing the responsibility on the victim for the threats they experience also occurs in Extract 67, where Alastair frames the victim's prior acts of blocking his messages as her being 'heartless' (line 2) and uses this to justify his subsequent threat to hurt her. He continues in his next turn to deliver an implicit threat by 'reminding' the victim that he has her 'home and work address' (line 3), which is detail that is often procured during the relationship under the guise of sending small gifts to the victim (gift-giving being a tactic also used to compel reciprocal giving, Whitty 2013) or to serve an exigent need (as seen in Extract 30).

Extract 67
1. Alastair: You block me 2 times from your whatsapp now i know you are very
2.   heartless i love you but i will hurt you more now
3. Alastair: i have you home and work address
4. Alastair: i make sure i post all your sex photos all over china and hong kong and
5.   even send to you mum and your family
6. Alastair: i will put some on you-tube, Facebook, and Instagram, twitter and
7.   micro now you have to pay for your freedom if you are ready to talk
8.   let me know
9. Alastair: I Alastair promise you that

Alastair engages in narratives of love, despite the romance having ended and he has begun calling her names. The discourse marker 'but' in his 'i love you but i will hurt you more now' (line 2) reflects the conflict between his stated love and his subsequent threat(s). The link between the victim's behaviour and his threats is suggested in his 'now you have to pay … ' (line 7), with the use of 'now' signalling a perspective shift and a change of state (moving from romancing the victim to threatening her, Lee 2017) as a result of the actions he highlights as problematic (line 1).

Using a combination of direct threats and indirect threats, Alastair balances indirect personal threat (knowing her home and work address, line 3) with the direct threat of the shame of her 'sex photos' (line 4) being seen by the public and her family. He focuses in on particular elements of both of these, two countries where she could be widely recognised (China and Hong Kong) and her mum (line 5, which is recognised as the most harmful through the use of 'even' as an intensifier). He then details the mechanisms through which this harm will be visited upon her, and frames this as a type of imprisonment through which she will never escape (as once the photos are published online, they remain in the virtual sphere indefinitely); by virtue of paying him, this would cease his actions, and this is framed by him as 'buying her freedom'. This phrase in itself is an act of direct extortion and is made more specific, removing any ambiguity about the threat through his promise in which, resembling a formal statement or contract of intent, he refers to himself when doing so (line 9).

Similar to Extract 67, the fraudster in Extract 68 uses his previously acquired knowledge of the victim's address as a mechanism through which to deliver threats, although in this case the threat of physical harm is more closely oriented to than in the previous extract ('bad people' are in her town, line 3). The 'remember' on line 1 explicitly orients the victim back to when he was communicating with her under the guise of a romance. Also similar to Extract 67, his use of her specific town (anonymised here) in his threat personalises it to her and therefore makes the threat specific and more tangible.

Extract 68

1.	F:	Remember I have your home address
2.		And I can make life a living heil [hell] for you
3.		I have so many bad people there in [TOWN].
4.		And 15 of you sex video
5.		I have 20 of your niked pix
6.		I also send some to your mom and family
7.		When am done I will make u famous in hk
8.		Then if you do that ready to face anything that
9.		Because u can't go anywhere
10.		Without people looking and u or calling u names
11.		Don't worry by the time I show you your house you know you have a lot to
12.		fear

He continues by delivering threats in relation to the 'sex video[s]' (line 4) and 'niked [naked] pix [pictures]' (line 5); the threat made personalised to the victim through the fraudster specifying the exact number of both types of intimate missive (fifteen and twenty, respectively; lines 4 and 5). This detail makes the prospect of the fraudster carrying out the threat appear more tangible and realistic, particularly given the practical prospect of the fraudster having invested time in searching through their interactions to count each photo and sex video the victim had sent him throughout their relationship; it is a reminder that he must have kept these and therefore has the tools to deliver the threat. The use of 'and' features in the turn-initial position on lines 2 and 4, with 'then' on line 8 a coordinating conjunction that links this back to the fraudster's opening, which make the turns appear as an outcome of, and logical progression of, the initial threat. The fraudster explicitly orients to the future impact of his actions on the victim, forecasting the shame associated with sending her videos and images to family and wider society in order to increase the leverage of his threat. This is also heightened implicitly with the discord between the passive 'don't worry' (line 11) and the threats before and after.

The physical threat associated with the fraudster knowing the victim's home address is used explicitly in Extract 69, where he threatens the victim with setting fire to her house (line 4). Similar to Extract 68, the fraudster personalises the threat by telling the victim that bad actors are in her (named) home town (line 1) and have been to her house that day (lines 1–2); this increases the immediacy of the threat in terms of reality (this can physically happen, with willing bad actors), temporality (it can happen at any time), and in terms of location (they are in my town). The threat is present, explicit, and geographically near.

Extract 69
1. F   I even have people in [TOWN] and I ask them to go check on your house
2.   today and they did
3.   You really don't know what you want to get yourself into
4.   If you take any wrong step I make sure I born [burn] down your house and
5.   you be in very big problem for that
6.   You think am joking right
7.   Okay I give you 3days to go look for the money after 3days I will do it
8.   I make sure I post your sex video to all your friends on facebook

Following the fraudster's set-up of the threat on line 4 with a warning ('if you take any wrong step', line 4) and the ensuing consequences (of burning her house down) of non-compliance, he then reveals the way in which the victim can prevent this from happening (find the money). The use of 'the' (line 7) in relation to this is important, as it shows the fraudster is demanding a specific amount of money that he has mentioned previously rather than money in general. Interestingly, the fraudster then issues the consequences for non-compliance, and rather than reiterating the previously set-up threat of arson, the fraudster then pivots from the physical threat to the victim's property (and by proxy, her life) to threatening to release her 'sex video' to her friends on Facebook (line 8).

Similar to Extracts 67 and 71, in Extract 70 the fraudster situates his threat of harm as in response to the (potential) harm visited on him by the victim; in this case, the victim 'tal[king] bad' (line 1) is presented as the act that would be reciprocated with him using her information to hurt her.

Extract 70
1. F: Don't just talk bad on me
2. F: Because if am hurt I can do you more bad
3. F: With your information

This frames the victim as responsible for her own fate, framing his anger and threats as a result of her responses and his actions as a result of her failing to act correctly; this is much like the discourses found in domestic violence and abuse (DVAB) of emotional abuse and responsibalising the victim for the psychological and physical harm that befalls them (Rakovec-Felser 2014).

In Extract 71, Dan blames Peggy for his business difficulties because she has not been able to send him what he considers to be enough money, and again we see the use of faux gratitude ('thanks a lot', line 1) which, in the context of the surrounding talk, takes on a passive aggressive form. He then weaponises the intimate photos he had previously coerced her into sending, using the threat of putting them online and showing them to her friends to compel her to send more money.

Extract 71
1. Dan: Thanks a lot the company just took back my order to warehouse
2. Dan: All this because I just let you into my business you fucked up my work for me
3. Dan: It shall not be well with you Penny
4. Dan: How would you feel if I showed your friends your naked pics
5. Dan: Or put it online

The 'let you' on line 2 suggests that Dan extended a level of trust to her in allowing her to get involved in his business, and it was because of this trust that he has experienced 'all this' (line 2) difficulty relating to his business; she is to blame because she squandered his good will. This is supported by the rest of the sentence, in which he explicitly states 'you fucked up my work for me' (line 2). In his next turn, Dan then forecasts the threat-to-come before delivering the threat, posed as a question about how she would feel if he showed the photos she had sent him during their relationship to her friends or posted them online (line 5). This is clearly a rhetorical question, as the prospect of this happening would undoubtedly be received with dread and an attempt to persuade the interlocutor to not do so.

The ferocity in which he pursues Peggy and accuses her reluctance to send him money as her harming his business is in direct contrast to his earlier interactions with her. In Extract 7, he advises her on 'being careful' about people asking for money online, while in Extract 26 he states that sharing a life with someone is more important than money, with money 'losinh meaning' without someone to share it with and that he would give it all up (line 21) for love. He also tells her, as part of a cautionary tale about fraudsters, that he himself ;Was talking with one woman earlier but she stopped talking to me because I refused to give her more money; Extract 7, lines 2–3). And yet later, when Peggy is in this same situation with him, he threatens her with the release of the intimate photos of her that he had persuaded her to send (Extract 35). This demonstrates the twisting of reality as the relationship progresses, and how even deeply contrasting claims and actions by the fraudster can be framed and mitigations delivered.

3 Discussion

This Element has exposed the romantic relationship itself as a resource that fraudsters draw on to increase the tools they have to leverage a range of requests of the victim, as well as showing how fraudsters handle challenges by victims. It has explored the interconnected nature of romance fraudsters' communicative techniques which adapt to, form, and mitigate transitions between the stages discovered in the romance fraud journey. These comprise Romance (relationship building), Transition (introducing and testing mitigations), Finance (the ask for money), and Post-romance (sextortion). The fraudsters' interactions are shown to be seamlessly adapted to accommodate the changing victim context: as romantic partner, protector, protected, collaborator, spouse, and compromised individual. This flexibility to manoeuvre through the stages of romance, transition, and finance, while maintaining the integrity of the romance, is facilitated by the fraudster's flexibility in projecting themselves variously as powerless, powerful, protective, and vulnerable. In enacting these personas, fraudsters rely on delivering promises and harnessing obligation; applying techniques of love bombing and trauma bombing; leveraging credibility and obligation; using promises; and turning to begging/demanding. The Element has revealed how these various personas manifest through the stages of romance fraud; they form into pairs where the second part (such as demanding the victim act through a sense of obligation) represents an escalation of the first (such as producing promises of love early in the relationship). Early in the fraud journey, the fraudster relies on the first of these pairs (promises, love bombing, begging), but as the journey moves through to the finance and beyond, into the post-romance stage, the fraudster uses the more explicit and direct second part of each pair (obligation, trauma bombing, demanding).

During the romance stage (Extracts 1–27), the fraudster needs to build rapport and establish credibility as a genuine love interest, someone safe and trustworthy. These are all established in both explicit and implicit ways in the romance stage. Vulnerability is used across the romance, transition, and finance stages, being as it is built on mimicking states of inexperience, hurt, and reliance to draw out a protective response from the victim and present a veneer of legitimacy. This is performed by the fraudster embodying a relatively powerless and imperfect persona that appears far from a confident and powerful manipulator. As part of this supposed vulnerability, fraudsters also position themselves as safe and a useful guide in terms of a genuine presence on the dating site. This is also explicitly achieved by them positioning themselves as the antithesis of a fraudster, topicalising *scamming* as a particular concern or occupational hazard when dating online, or as the 'other' that they explicitly draw attention to in terms of cautionary tales and protecting the victim.

Trustworthiness is also introduced in a more direct way. In doing so, the fraudster produces scripts in relation to their characteristics and the behaviours and characteristics expected of the victim, such as loyalty and honesty. These ostensibly flattering (both for the fraudster and the victim) accounts of their own personality (fraudster) and that of their ideal partner (the victim) are presented as part of rapport building and information exchange that is embedded in the contextual norms of budding relationships. The importance of the right partner and their own position as a good future prospect is reflected in the fraudster's casual approach to commitment until they are comfortable; this apparent choosiness reinforces their credibility as a genuine dating site user rather than a fraudster intent on defrauding someone. The use of religion is also present, where a higher being is used in some cases as the driver of the relationship which both parties should defer to and live up to in terms of behaviour and joint expectations to stay committed to the success of the relationship. It is at this point that fraudsters establish norms and expectations that they will later rely on to frame the request as normal or as a tool to directly convince the victim to comply. Within this structure we can see the first of many two-pair parts of the fraudster's toolkit; the fraudster's promises produced in the romance stage return in the finance and sextortion stages, having morphed into the victim's obligation.

The overarching areas in which fraudsters set up behaviours and qualities that can later be exploited are reciprocal and mutual assistance and support, and problem-solving. The fraudster's expectations of the victim's behaviour, cast in the romance stage as the characteristics of their ideal partner, then re-emerge as the fraudster's disappointment at the victim not living up to their expectations and betraying earlier promises. Before entering the finance stage (Extracts 52–65), where the victim is asked for money, the fraudster first needs to ensure that they maintain that rapport and engagement with the victim they have built within the framework of the romantic relationship, in order to avoid causing the victim alarm which could lead them to abandon the relationship (as seen in Extract 61). This, the transition stage (Extracts 28–51) acts as a buffer between romance and finance and enables the otherwise concerning practice of asking for money to be mitigated. During the transition stage, fraudsters rely on contextual support to enable the facade to continue throughout the transition from romantic talk to matters relating to money. This involves normalising and romanticising risk-taking, normalising secrecy, and romanticising choosing love over money. The personalisation to the victim's circumstances and context also increases the likelihood of compliance (Modic and Lea 2013).

Scripting is used to ease the transition between the romance and finance stages by forecasting and addressing future potentially concerning elements. This is performed implicitly rather than explicitly in order for it to make sense within the context of romance, with the fraudster's discourse, heavy as it is with implicature, delivered as a reflection about risk-taking and sacrifices within the wider narrative of ideal partners rather than a direct request for the victim to take risks or make financial sacrifices. These narratives, however, much like other scripting performed in the romance and transition stages, are later used to mitigate requests of the victim to perform risky activities (such as intimate communications) or those that will involve them sacrificing their money or personal information. Risk-reduction strategies are present across all stages of the romance fraud, from the illusion of agency in the early romance, the vulnerability and joint responsibility in transition to the reframing and down-playing of requests in the finance stage.

Mitigations of otherwise concerning requests, when they manifest as normal-isations through performance-as-request, can serve to not only *protect* the existing facade of the relationship (avoiding a 'reassurance void' which would open the interaction to questioning) but to also *increase* the credibility of the fraudster's situation or the credibility of the fraudster themselves, while isolating the victim. This is shown in fraudsters compelling secrecy through the performance of secrecy themselves, inviting reciprocal intimate communications both implicitly and explicitly, and through harnessing the romantic context and attendant expectations.

Mitigations can occur throughout the romance, transition, and finance stages, in terms of the fraudster managing their own denials of victim requests to meet or to interact via video call or telephone. Also, moving beyond the two interactants, the fraudster draws on the wider context in terms of other characters; they frame requests as a requirement of others that is beyond their control, as shown in requests for personal information framed as a safety requirement. This distances the fraudster from the responsibility and ownership of the request, lending it credibility as it comes from external sources (Carter 2015). The fraudster also expresses unhappiness and frustration at these requirements. Instead of showering the victim in declarations of love and increased affection after a concerning situation has occurred, or as seen in early stages of the relationship (love bombing), the fraudster engages in trauma bombing, in another example of a two-pair part; one tactic has a counterpart that is used in a later stage of the fraud. Trauma bombing occurs in the transition, finance, and post-romance sextortion stages, at points where victim concerns are raised or requests the fraudster cannot service are made. It serves multiple purposes – concealing the fraudster as the real source of the refusal or denial of victim requests and positioning the fraudster as being harmed alongside the victim. The facade of joint harm enhances the connection between victim and fraudster, as seen in trauma bonding, which is so powerful it makes it difficult for women to leave abusive relationships (Hadeed 2021). This positions the fraudster as suffering (more than the victim) and mitigates the fraudster's inability to agree to the victim's requests. It moves the victim away from topicalising what is being said and abandoning or quashing their own disappointment for fear of distressing the fraudster.

This is where another pair part is present: the cultivation of credibility that dominates the romance stage appears substituted for obligation. During the finance stage, the fraudster will seek to offset requests for money by elevating the victim's status in the relationship and their relationship more broadly. Fraudsters transform earlier stated expectations into obligations or requirements around requests for money, (re)framing money-giving as expected behaviour (sometimes with explicit links to the earlier set-up and scripting stages), or as a duty to be fulfilled by the victim as part of their gender role or the specific role they hold in the relationship (supposed husband/wife/trusted partner). Other mitigations include visceral responses, which are harnessed by the fraudster to draw a protective response from the victim (Carter 2021). If the victim's protective response doesn't take the form of offering financial assistance, the fraudster then steers the victim towards this, and this is where we can see the third pair part, where the promising from the early stage of the relationship transitions to begging. Later, when the relationship ends and moves into sextortion, we then see this transform yet again to the fraudster issuing demands.

As the fraudster moves the victim through to the finance stage, the faux vulnerabilities shown by the fraudster become more explicit and more frequent. By displaying reticent vulnerability in financial requests, fraudsters isolate victims within a context of framing them as the only person they have revealed their financial difficulties to or as the only person that can help, complete with the implicit potential for embarrassment if anyone else knew the fraudster's difficult situation. Once one tactic is successful, the fraudster will then work to maintain this success across as many moments of money-taking as possible. This is achieved through reharnessing requests under the premise of 'just another', 'the same again', or 'one last/final payment', until the fraudster manoeuvres to a different tactic. The finance stage also encompasses fraudsters' requests for photos of the victim and establishing of intimate conversations, as these can occur concurrently and both signify the movement of the interaction away from romance, although requests are framed using that context. The fraudster steers conversations towards intimacy and harnesses reciprocal intimate talk and photo exchange, but also leverages wider societal norms and expectations of reciprocation and intimacy in relationships. If this doesn't succeed, the fraudster will draw on visceral responses while levelling accusations of failure of trust (or similar) at victims who refuse or challenge requests for personal details or photos.

The analyses reveal that urgency is used in fraudulent talk and is usually present during requests for money or to facilitate victim compliance with an act that leads to their exposure to financial harm. It is not usually seen in communications preceding this, as it is used to drive urgent action, something which would be incongruous in early stages of 'establishing credibility and trust', 'building rapport', and 'forecasting and romanticising future behaviours' and therefore their later use cannot be mitigated through early exposure. During the transition and finance stages of the communication, the victim may become alarmed and challenge the fraudster; such challenges are met with reciprocal challenges where fraudsters will redirect the victim's concern to 'expose' *their* substandard level of commitment or trust. Leveraging and weaponising the content of earlier interactions occurs during the finance stage; we see this most explicitly where the fraudster's scripting in the romance stage is revisited and reframed as disappointment against hopes and expectations, often manifesting as a visceral response. This type of response serves to disguise the issue of contention within a reverse reality where the victim is at fault (mirroring tactics in domestic abuse). This shows the shift from language that empowers the victim in the early stages of the relationship to language that overpowers the victim; the fraudster uses disappointment to coerce the victim into action, something that then becomes more direct post-romance. Direct threats in the post-romance stage include faux gratitude, victim blaming, deferral to a higher power, anchoring threats to real information and situations, and forecasts of physical and social harm. This 'future-proofing' occurs in both guarding the relationship for changes in status (from romantic to financial) and also in preparing for the move from finance to sextortion by gathering data such as the victim's home address, intimate messaging, and intimate photos through which to leverage for money.

The weaponising of information and content derived through the course of the relationship seen in the transition and finance stages reoccurs during the sextortion phase in explicit and direct form, in terms of threats to the victim's safety and privacy. Instead of manipulating earlier interactions to invoke that talk as future promises and coerce the victim into complying with requests, in the post-romance stage it is the intimate images and messages gathered *and kept* during the course of the 'healthy' relationship that are used against the victim to directly extort money from them. This contradicts prior understandings of sextortion in the context of romance fraud, where it is said images are demanded from romance fraud victims after the relationship has ended or shortly prior to this (Whitty 2015); they are coerced from the victim and then acted upon as quickly as possible to defraud them (Anesa 2020). The work in this Element clearly shows a different type of sextortion, defined and assisted by the context of romance. Outside of romance fraud, in traditional sextortion, demands are made of the victim immediately upon receipt of the sexually explicit images or video (Tampubolon 2023). This is also seen as such by Anesa (2020: 2), who notes that '[romance fraud] and sextortion can be part of the same fraudulent attempt and may of course coexist and overlap, and the former in some cases, can lead to the latter', although, crucially, sextortion is again defined as an immediate 'gotcha', where victims, upon sending explicit material, are immediately confronted with demands to pay to keep the material secret. Traditional sextortion centres around images and videos; romance fraud enabled sextortion also includes intimate and sexual messages, and the exposure of the relationship itself is used as a weapon. Traditional sextortion involves demands for money, but can also leverage already-obtained explicit images or videos to coerce the victim into sending further images or videos (Tampubolon 2023), particularly in the case of female victims who are more likely to be in a (fraudulent) relationship with the perpetrator than their male counterparts who have limited contact with the perpetrator prior to the crime (Cross, Holt, and O'Malley 2022). With romance fraud enabled sextortion, the weaponised explicit content is procured solely for financial gain following the failure of the romance fraud financial abuse pipeline. Also, rather than a tool of escalation (Button and Cross 2017), sextortion is more of a 'back-up' that is prepared for well in advance of when the relationship has ceased to yield money from the victim or has otherwise ended.

4 Conclusion

Although there appear to be almost limitless combinations of possible paths of discussion between fraudster and victim, multiplied many times over due to individual responses, contexts, and decisions which themselves then precipitate a whole other range of responses, decisions, and contexts, this Element has laid bare the broad structure and overarching range of touchpoints and potential roadblocks that must be navigated by criminals throughout their attempt to defraud an individual through the facade of a romantic relationship. These are certain points that need to be successfully crossed without causing the victim alarm in order for the fraud to begin and continue unhindered throughout stories and rationales that lead to the 'ask for money'. The ask itself and also the associated secrecy, isolation, and scripting are needed in the performance of money-giving and the maintenance of the facade (which is at risk when those outside of the interaction are able to spot it and warn the victim). By situating these communications within the normal or expected framework of a developing romantic relationship, as an indication of trust, love, and sincerity, or as an unfortunate technicality, issue with technology, or requirement of another party, the fraudster can account for situations that require them to request secrecy, urgency, and the refusal of acts that will enable the victim to verify their identity (such as meeting or video calls). Indeed, by leveraging the relationship, expectations, or an event that, in itself, requires support from the other interactant, the otherwise concerning requirements to act urgently, in secret, or being unable to meet or communicate visually themselves become legitimised as a reasonable response to the situation. The escalation of behaviours along the romance fraud journey reflect the increasing exploitation of the victim in the move towards explicit threat, something facilitated only by the manipulation of the early stages of the romance; this is an essential insight for organisations and practitioners to ensure is reflected in public protection information. This escalation is operationalised by the first part of the pair (delivering promises turns into harnessing obligation; love bombing morphs into trauma bombing; leveraging credibility moves to leveraging obligation; and early promises move into the fraudster begging, and, later, demanding). There are clear links between romance fraud and the language used in coercive control and domestic violence and abuse in each stage of the journey. Distorting victim requests and blaming the victim are present in the latter stages of the relationship, in relation to responding to victims challenging the fraudster or refusing to comply with requests (and beyond, into the post-romance interaction). More implicit or hidden manipulations are present in the earlier stages, seen in setting out the ideal partner and responsibalising the victim. Vulnerability appears as a key mechanism of manipulation in the form of false self-reports of inexperience, distress from prior hurt, reliance, lack of power, self-deprecation, and cautiousness. Compelling loyalty and obedience as a key tactic of fraud discourse adds to and moves understandings of manipulation and coercion beyond intimidation-based acts (Stark 2012) and highlights the particular nuance of coercive behaviour within the context of a romance fraud. Crucially, this examination of the 'romance fraud journey' has revealed that sextortion is *built into* the romance fraud in terms of the fraud being used as the means to procure the tools needed to sextort the victim later and is not a separate or detached criminality.

Fraudsters occupy online dating spaces in a way that is not obvious and is not recognised as odd behaviour, and it offers a false sense of security to individuals in that space that they are safe. This is part of the reason why romance fraud is so pervasive and remains undetected by its victims early on because these normalised interactions are ones where information and details about the other party is perfect for a criminal intent on defrauding them. The high crime rate and low reporting rate demands that academics and practitioners cannot continue to attempt to explain victimhood in narrow terms of personal vulnerability, financial loss, and special cases. This is because it disguises the reality of fraud as a type of abuse and misrepresents victims as having done something for the crime to be visited upon them, which in turn drives negative narratives of victims of fraud and perpetuates a victim-blaming culture against them. The skewed perception of fraud and fraud victims is reflected in the presence of victims that have an over-confidence in their ability to spot fraud, with this linked to their opinion of their own intellect in relation to the person contacting them, a phenomenon termed 'the better-than-average effect' (Alicke and Govorun 2005). Fraudulent requests for money are also (mis)framed in public protection information as easily identifiable as concerning – termed here the 'red flag phenomenon'. The general public are warned to be aware of demands for money when they are unexpected ('out of the blue'), incongruous ('don't give money to someone who you just met'), or problematically positive ('if it seems too good to be true, it probably is'). However not only are these states practically impossible to definitively define, they also don't reflect the modus operandi of romance fraud; rather, they are typically found in '419 scams', otherwise known as 'Nigerian Prince emails' that are designed to be so obvious to most that only a small number of people will respond, and of those, most will lose money. Romance fraud victims therefore suffer a double difficulty – the ways they can identify this type of fraud are misrepresented by conflating this crime with other, non-grooming-based frauds, so they are unable to use public protection advice to identify a fraudulent relationship and take steps to protect themselves. Also, when individuals become victim to romance fraud, public perceptions are that they are at fault by not adequately protecting themselves from what is depicted as an obvious 'trick' or 'swindle'. This belies the development of the relationship, the process through which perpetrators of this crime groom their victims into a position that, by the time the 'ask for money' occurs, is entirely normalised, mitigated, and non-concerning. When talk turns to money, it is rarely a 'demand'; rather, it is innocuous and credible in the context of what appears to be a healthy, normal online relationship. It is often heavily disguised or mitigated by seating it within contextually credible discursive frameworks, which I term 'genre mapping' (Carter 2015). By representing fraud as easily identifiable, and victimhood styled as preventable through engaging in a small number of simple self-protection steps, the organisations whose job it is to protect the public are inadvertently increasing public vulnerability to fraud and adding to the public narrative and perceptions that victims of fraud have not protected themselves adequately.

Victims that have been a victim of romance fraud and then become a further victim of sextortion, blackmail, or other direct threats will likely not report the crime as they experience additional feelings of shame, compounded in terms of admitting the intimate nature of the interactions they have had with a criminal who had tricked them into so doing. The shame of what they have been manipulated into sending the fraudster is also weaponised, with the fraudster using the threat of exposure as the driver through which to extort money. Other direct threats involve weaponising knowledge of the victim's home or work address, or address of their childrens' school, which they can use to threaten physical violence unless their financial demands are met, and done so without alerting the authorities; the victim's physical safety and psychological well-being are effectively held to ransom.

The act of capturing intimate messages and images, requests protected under the guise of a healthy and developing relationship, with intent to weaponise these at a later stage as tools to demand money from the victim at a later stage is one of the most insidious yet under-researched elements of romance fraud. This Element lays bare the reality of romance fraud as an intricate interplay between love, money, and threat, and as a conduit for further criminal acts. It has revealed and explored the presence of a separate type of sextortion, '*romance fraud enabled sextortion*', that is different from traditional definitions of sextortion in modus operandi. As a consequence of this, current legal distinctions between 'fraud' and 'kidnap and extortion' that house romance fraud and sextortion separately and distinctly can disguise the presence and risk of sextortion within fraudulent encounters. Therefore, this can leave victims of romance fraud unalert to these potential threats, unprotected from harm, and unable to accurately report these through existing channels that artificially silo the crimes.

In exposing the reality of the progressive interactional tactics of grooming and manipulation that victims of romance fraud experience, this Element provides essential insights into and understanding of romance fraud that can be used to improve public protection efforts, police response to it, and victim aftercare. The impacts of this Element include directly informing the creation of accurate, effective messaging and information to protect the public from becoming victim to romance fraud. The Element's contributions also extend to influencing a societal reimagining of perceptions of victims of this crime, as well as aligning romance fraud with crimes of abuse and extortion, in terms of crime type, severity, harm, long-term impacts, reporting support, and victim care needs.

References

Action Fraud (2023a). 'Advance Fee'. www.actionfraud.police.uk/a-z-of-fraud-category/advance-fee.

Action Fraud (2023b). 'Advance Fee Fraud'. www.actionfraud.police.uk/a-z-of-fraud/advance-fee-fraud.

Action Fraud (2023c). 'Fraud Recovery Fraud'. www.actionfraud.police.uk/a-z-of-fraud/fraud-recovery-fraud.

Alicke, M. D. and Govorun, O. (2005). 'The Better-Than-Average Effect'. In M. D. Alicke, D. A. Dunning, and J. I. Krueger (Eds.), *The Self in Social Judgment* (pp. 85–106). London: Psychology Press.

Anesa, P. (2020). 'Lovextortion: Persuasion Strategies in Romance Fraud'. *Discourse, Context and Media* 35: 1–8. https://doi.org/10.1016/j.dcm.2020.100398.

Buchanan, T. and Whitty, M. T. (2013). 'The Online Dating Romance Scam: Causes and Consequences of Victimhood'. *Psychology, Crime & Law* 20: 261–83.

Button, M. and Cross, C. (2017). *Cyber Frauds, Scams and Their Victims*. London: Taylor & Francis.

Button, M., Lewis, C., and Tapley, J. (2009). *A Better Deal for Fraud Victims: Research into Victims' Needs and Experiences*. London: National Fraud Authority. https://researchportal.port.ac.uk/portal/files/1924328/NFA_Report_1_15.12.09.pdf.

Button, M., Lewis, C., and Tapley, J. (2014). 'Not a Victimless Crime: The Impact of Fraud on Individual Victims and Their Families'. *Security Journal* 27(1): 36–54. https://doi.org/10.1057/sj.2012.11.

Campbell, J. C., Webster, D., Koziol-McLain, J. et al. (2003). 'Risk Factors for Femicide in Abusive Relationships: Results From a Multisite Case Control Study'. *American Journal of Public Health* 93: 1089–97. https://doi.org/10.2105/AJPH.93.7.1089.

Carter, E. (2015). 'The Anatomy of Scam Communications: An Empirical Analysis'. *Crime, Media, Culture* 11: 89–103.

Carter, E. (2021). 'Distort, Extort, Deceive and Exploit: Exploring the Inner Workings of a Romance Fraud'. *The British Journal of Criminology* 61(2): 283–302. https://doi.org/10.1093/bjc/azaa072.

Carter, E. (2023). 'Confirm Not Command: Examining Fraudsters' Use of Language to Compel Victim Compliance in Their Own Exploitation'. *The British Journal of Criminology* 63(6): 1405–22. https://doi.org/10.1093/bjc/azac098.

Clift, R. (2001). 'Meaning in Interaction: The Case of Actually'. *Language* 77(2): 245–91. www.jstor.org/stable/3086775.

CrimeStoppers (2023). 'Romance Fraud'. https://crimestoppers-uk.org/keeping-safe/fraud/romance-fraud.

Crime Survey for England and Wales (2019). 'Nature of Fraud and Computer Misuse in England and Wales: Year Ending March 2019'. www.ons.gov.uk/peoplepopulationandcommunity/crimeandjustice/articles/natureoffraudandcomputermisuseinenglandandwales/yearendingmarch2019#fraud-reporting-to-action-fraud.

Cross, C. (2015). 'No Laughing Matter: Blaming the Victim of Online Fraud'. *International Review of Victimology* 21: 187–204.

Cross, C. (2016). '"They're Very Lonely": Understanding the Fraud Victimisation of Seniors'. *International Journal for Crime, Justice and Social Democracy* 5(4): 60–75. https://search.informit.org/doi/10.3316/agispt.20172306.

Cross, C. and Lee, M. (2022). 'Exploring Fear of Crime for Those Targeted by Romance Fraud'. *Victims & Offenders* 17(5): 735–55. https://doi.org/10.1080/15564886.2021.2018080.

Cross, C., Holt, K., and O'Malley, R. L. (2022). '"If U Don't Pay They Will Share the Pics": Exploring Sextortion in the Context of Romance Fraud'. *Victims & Offenders* 18: 1194–1215. https://doi.org/10.1080/15564886.2022.2075064.

Cross, C., Smith, R. G., and Richards, K. (2014). *Trends and Issues in Crime and Criminal Justice: Challenges of Responding to Online Fraud Victimisation in Australia*. Canberra: Australian Institute of Criminology, Australian Government. https://eprints.qut.edu.au/72186/1/tandi474.pdf.

Crown Prosecution Service (2023). 'Controlling or Coercive Behaviour in an Intimate or Family Relationship'. www.cps.gov.uk/legal-guidance/controlling-or-coercive-behaviour-intimate-or-family-relationship.

Domestic Abuse Act 2021, s1. www.legislation.gov.uk/ukpga/2021/17/part/1/enacted.

Dove, M. (2020). *The Psychology of Fraud, Persuasion and Scam Techniques: Understanding What Makes Us Vulnerable*. London: Routledge.

Fenge, L. and Lee, S. (2018). 'Understanding the Risks of Financial Scams as Part of Elder Abuse Prevention'. *British Journal of Social Work* 48: 906–23.

Fitzpatrick, S. J., Brew, B. K., Handley, T., and Perkins, D. (2022). 'Men, Suicide, and Family and Interpersonal Violence: A Mixed Methods Exploratory Study'. *Sociology of Health & Illness* 44(6): 991–1008. https://doi.org/10.1111/1467-9566.13476.

Fraud Act 2006, s2. www.legislation.gov.uk/ukpga/2006/35/pdfs/ukpga_20060035_en.pdf.

Freiermuth, M. R. (2011). 'Text, Lies and Electronic Bait: An Analysis of Email Fraud and the Decisions of the Unsuspecting'. *Discourse and Communication* 5(2): 123–45.

Giles, H. (2009). 'The Process of Communication Accommodation'. In N. Coupland and A. Jaworski (Eds.), *The New Sociolinguistics Reader* (pp. 276–86). London: Palgrave Macmillan.

Gov.uk (2021). 'Fraud, Tricks and Scams: Guidance'. www.gov.uk/govern ment/publications/frauds-tricks-and-scams/fraud-tricks-and-scams.

Hadeed, L. (2021). 'Why Women Stay: Understanding the Trauma Bond Between Victim and Abuser Case Studies Were Written'. In A. M. Bissessar and C. Huggins (Eds.), *Gender and Domestic Violence in the Caribbean: Gender, Development and Social Change* (pp. 195–207). Cham: Palgrave Macmillan. https://doi.org/10.1007/978-3-030-73472-5_12.

Harrington, L. (2018) '"Helping You to Pay Us": Rapport Management in Debt Collection Call Centre Encounters'. *Journal of Politeness Research* 14(2): 193–223. https://doi.org/10.1515/pr-2018-0013.

Hawkswood, J., Carter, E., and Brown, K. (2022). 'Coercion and Control in Financial Abuse: Learning from Domestic Abuse'. National Trading Standards (NTS) Scams Team. www.shropshiresafeguardingcommunitypart nership.co.uk/media/opgnzfx0/carter-brown-and-hawkswood-2022-ntsst-financial-fraud-coercion-and-control-report.pdf.

Heritage, J. (1984). *Garfinkel and Ethnomethodology*. Cambridge: Polity Press.

Hill, J. (2020). *See What You Made Me Do: Power, Control and Domestic Abuse*. London: Hurst Publishers.

House of Lords (2022). Fraud Act 2006 and Digital Fraud Committee HL Paper 87. 'Fighting Fraud: Breaking the Chain'. https://publications.parliament.uk/pa/ld5803/ldselect/ldfraudact/87/87.pdf.

Judges, R. A., Gallant, S. N., Yang, L., and Lee, K. (2017). 'The Role of Cognition, Personality, and Trust in Fraud Victimization in Older Adults'. *Frontiers in Psychology* 13(8): 1–10. https://doi.org/10.3389/fpsyg.2017.00588.

Kennedy, J. P., Rorie, M., and Benson, M. L. (2021). 'COVID-19 Frauds: An Exploratory Study of Victimisation during a Global Crisis'. *Criminology & Public Policy* 20: 493–543. https://doi.org/10.1111/1745-9133.12554.

Koon, T. H. and Yoong, D. (2013). 'Preying on Lonely Hearts: A Systematic Deconstruction of an Internet Romance Scammer's Online Lover Persona'. *Journal of Modern Languages* 23: 28–40.

Lea, S., Fischer, P., and Evans, K. (2009). *The Psychology of Scams: Provoking and Committing Errors of Judgement*. Report for the Office of Fair Trading. Exeter: University of Exeter School of Psychology. https://webarchive.natio

nalarchives.gov.uk/20140402205717/http://oft.gov.uk/shared_oft/reports/consumer_protection/oft1070.pdf.

Lee, E. (2017). 'Discourse Properties of Now'. *Journal of Linguistics* 53(3): 613–40. https://doi.org/10.1017/S0022226715000432.

Mesch, G. S. and Beker, G. (2010). 'Are Norms of Disclosure of Online and Offline Personal Information Associated with the Disclosure of Personal Information Online?' *Human Communication Research* 36(4): 570–92. https://doi.org/10.1111/j.1468-2958.2010.01389.x.

Metropolitan Police (2023). 'Cyber Crime'. www.met.police.uk/advice/advice-and-information/fa/fraud/online-fraud/cyber-crime-fraud/.

Modic, D. and Lea, S. E. G. (2013). 'Scam Compliance and the Psychology of Persuasion'. Social Science Research Network. http://dx.doi.org/10.2139/ssrn.2364464.

National Crime Agency (NCA) (2023). 'Sextortion (Webcam Blackmail)'. https://nationalcrimeagency.gov.uk/what-we-do/crime-threats/kidnap-and-extortion/sextortion-webcam-blackmail.

Nilsson, M. G., Tzani-Pepelasis, C., Ioannou, M., and Lester, D. (2019). 'Understanding the Link between Sextortion and Suicide'. *International Journal of Cyber Criminology* 13(1): 55–69. https://doi.org/10.5281/zenodo.3402357.

O'Malley, R. L. (2023). 'Short-Term and Long-Term Impacts of Financial Sextortion on Victim's Mental Well-Being'. *Journal of Interpersonal Violence* 38(13–14): 8563–92. https://doi.org/10.1177/08862605231156416.

Offei, M., Andoh-Baidoo, F. K., Ayaburi, E. W., and Asamoah, D. (2022). 'How Do Individuals Justify and Rationalize Their Criminal Behaviors in Online Romance Fraud?'. *Information Systems Frontiers* 24: 475–91. https://doi.org/10.1007/s10796-020-10051-2.

Pomerantz, A. M. and Heritage, J. (2013). 'Preference'. In J. Sidnell and T. Stivers (Eds.), *Handbook of Conversation Analysis* (pp. 210–28). New York: Wiley-Blackwell.

Rakovec-Felser, Z. (2014). 'Domestic Violence and Abuse in Intimate Relationship from Public Health Perspective'. *Health Psychology Research* 2(3): 62–7. https://doi.org/10.4081/hpr.2014.1821.

Tampubolon, M. (2023). 'Digital Face Forgery and the Role of Digital Forensics'. *International Journal for the Semiotics of Law*. https://doi.org/10.1007/s11196-023-10030-1.

Serious Crime Act 2015, s76. www.legislation.gov.uk/ukpga/2015/9/section/76/2015-12-29.

Spencer-Oatey, H. (2002). 'Managing Rapport in Talk: Using Rapport Sensitive Incidents to Explore the Motivational Concerns Underlying the Management of Relations'. *Journal of Pragmatics* 34(5): 529–45. https://doi.org/10.1016/S0378-2166(01)00039-X.

Stark, E. (2012). 'Looking Beyond Domestic Violence: Policing Coercive Control'. *Journal of Police Crisis Negotiations* 12(2): 199–217. https://doi.org/10.1080/15332586.2012.725016.

Strutzenberg, C. (2016). 'Love-Bombing: A Narcissistic Approach to Relationship Formation'. Human Development and Family Sciences Undergraduate Honors Thesis, University of Arkansas. https://scholarworks.uark.edu/hdfsrsuht/1.

Sussex Police (2023). 'Romance Fraud'. www.sussex.police.uk/romance-fraud.

The National Lottery (1997). 'It Could Be You'. www.youtube.com/watch?v=J_yiuJ0ZM44.

Thomee, S., Eklof, M., Gustafson, E., Nilsson, R., and Hagberg, M. (2007). 'Prevalence of Perceived Stress, Symptoms of Depression and Sleep Disturbances in Relation to Information and Communication Technology (ICT) Use Among Young Adults – An Explorative Prospective Study'. *Computers in Human Behavior* 23: 1300–21. https://doi.org/10.1016/j.chb.2004.12.007.

Victim Support (2023). 'Domestic Abuse'. www.victimsupport.org.uk/crime-info/types-crime/domestic-abuse/.

Walsh, W. A. and Tener, D. (2022). '"If You Don't Send Me Five Other Pictures I Am Going to Post the Photo Online": A Qualitative Analysis of Experiences of Survivors of Sextortion'. *Journal of Child Sexual Abuse* 31(4): 447–65. https://doi.org/10.1080/10538712.2022.2067093.

Wang, F. and Topalli, V. (2022). 'Understanding Romance Scammers Through the Lens of Their Victims: Qualitative Modeling of Risk and Protective Factors in the Online Context'. American Journal of Criminal Justice (2022). https://doi.org/10.1007/s12103-022-09706-4.

Whitty, M. T. (2015). 'Anatomy of the Online Dating Romance Scam'. *Security Journal* 28: 443–55. https://doi.org/10.1057/sj.2012.57.

Whitty, M. T. (2018). 'Do You Love Me? Psychological Characteristics of Romance Scam Victims'. *Cyberpsychology, Behavior and Social Networking* 21(2): 105–9.

Whitty, M. T. and Buchanan, T. (2016). 'The Online Dating Romance Scam: The Psychological Impact on Victims – Both Financial and Non-financial. *Criminology & Criminal Justice* 16(2): 176–94. https://doi.org/10.1177/1748895815603773.

Whitty, M. T. (2013). 'The Scammers Persuasive Techniques Model: Development of a Stage Model to Explain the Online Dating Romance

Scam'. *The British Journal of Criminology* 53(4): 665–84 https://doi.org/10.1093/bjc/azt009.

Yuxi, S., Zhongxian, W., Xiaoyu, D. et al. (2022). 'The Psychology of the Internet Fraud Victimization of Older Adults: A Systematic Review'. *Frontiers in Psychology* 13. https://doi.org/10.3389/fpsyg.2022.912242.

Cambridge Elements ☰

Forensic Linguistics

Tim Grant
Aston University

Tim Grant is Professor of Forensic Linguistics, Director of the Aston Institute for Forensic Linguistics, and past president of the International Association of Forensic Linguists. His recent publications have focussed on online sexual abuse conversations including *Language and Online Identities: The Undercover Policing of Internet Sexual Crime* (with Nicci MacLeod, Cambridge, 2020).

Tim is one of the world's most experienced forensic linguistic practitioners and his case work has involved the analysis of abusive and threatening communications in many different contexts including investigations into sexual assault, stalking, murder, and terrorism. He also makes regular media contributions including presenting police appeals such as for the BBC *Crimewatch* programme.

Tammy Gales
Hofstra University

Tammy Gales is an Associate Professor of Linguistics and the Director of Research at the Institute for Forensic Linguistics, Threat Assessment, and Strategic Analysis at Hofstra University, New York. She has served on the Executive Committee for the International Association of Forensic Linguists (IAFL), is on the editorial board for the peer-reviewed journals *Applied Corpus Linguistics* and *Language and Law / Linguagem e Direito*, and is a member of the advisory board for the BYU Law and Corpus Linguistics group. Her research interests cross the boundaries of forensic linguistics and language and the law, with a primary focus on threatening communications. She has trained law enforcement agents from agencies across Canada and the U.S. and has applied her work to both criminal and civil cases.

About the Series

Elements in Forensic Linguistics provides high-quality accessible writing, bringing cutting-edge forensic linguistics to students and researchers as well as to practitioners in law enforcement and law. Elements in the series range from descriptive linguistics work, documenting a full range of legal and forensic texts and contexts; empirical findings and methodological developments to enhance research, investigative advice, and evidence for courts; and explorations into the theoretical and ethical foundations of research and practice in forensic linguistics.

Cambridge Elements ≡

Forensic Linguistics

Printed in the United States
by Baker & Taylor Publisher Services